The
Psychology of Conducting

Peter Paul Fuchs

MCA MUSIC. A division of MCA Inc.

Preface

Conducting is a much discussed subject in our days. Many young musicians decide that they want to be conductors, or at least that they would like to learn as much as possible about conducting. Some do it out of genuine talent and inclination, others for a variety of the wrong reasons. There are musicians whose severely limited proficiency on their instruments causes them to look for a specialization which in their opinion is easier and more promising of success; some who feel that sooner or later they may be asked to lead a musical ensemble, and that they had better be prepared for it; and still others who have no better justification to offer than an inborn desire to be in command. As a result, much is being done to help these candidates in their first bungling steps: courses are being taught, many of them quite bad, and books are being written, most of them quite good. In fact, it is surprising that on such a complex subject there should exist a wealth of printed material which presents in a concise and comprehensible manner at least a major portion of what is teachable, offering valuable assistance where inexperienced teachers often may fall far short of their intended goal.

With all this printed material readily available, headed by the books of Hermann Scherchen and Max Rudolf that are now considered classics, and a great many others, mostly of more recent origin, what is the justification for yet another book on the subject of conducting?

For one thing, this is not a textbook. It purposely avoids all problems of basic technique, offers no diagrams or beating patterns, does not discuss the execution of rests, holds or cutoffs. It concentrates, as the title explains, on problems of a psychological nature. (Let it be stated here without equivocation that the term "psychology" is used in its popular rather than in its scientific sense — since the author is not a trained psychologist, he does not intend to lay claim to a psychologically scientific approach!). These problems which must be faced at every step, as soon as the confrontation between the conductor and the smallest ensemble of live musicians begins, have — to the best of my knowledge — been dealt with only in a rather perfunctory fashion in most of the books. Much of the space quite understandably has been devoted to the development of a physical technique, and only very little to what happens after this technique has been developed to a reasonable degree — when it is to be put to the test in front of an orchestra. And yet it happens quite frequently that the student who has passed his final conducting exam with flying colors (with the instructor playing the piano), or who can brilliantly conduct Stravinsky's *Sacre* to the sounds of a record player, will fail miserably in his first attempt to conduct a small string ensemble in Mozart's *Eine kleine Nachtmusik*! He has finished his studies, but he is still worlds away from being a competent conductor!

Evidently there must be a gap somewhere, a gap between the commonly taught technique of conducting and the actual demands of leading a live orchestra. Obviously this gap can be reduced by giving the student practical opportunities to conduct, but such opportunities are of necessity quite limited. The gap has been recognized, yet in many cases its existence is brushed off with one word: experience! This is supposedly a cure-all: "You may not be able to do this now — just wait until you have gained some practical experience!" Sometimes it is hard to fight this statement, for it happens to be at least partially true: experience will teach even the conductor of limited endowment how to cope with difficult situations. In European theatres we find many "seasoned" conductors who are no masters in any sense but who somehow always manage to "get through" without a major accident.

The method seems to work, but at what cost! Is it fair to subject a large group of professional musicians to the more or less bungling attempts of a well meaning fledgling who may know exactly where every beat should be, who may even have memorized the score, but who is still unaware of the *real* problems of conducting? Moreover, is it fair to the young man himself, who will have to endure chuckles or worse from a group of hardened individuals who on this occasion may be more sensitive to wasting their own time than to the problems of the newcomer? Unless he happens to have the resilient personality of a Toscanini or a Kleiber, how long will it take his ego to recuperate from these blows? Or will it ever? . . .

Naturally, the gap will always exist. This is the basic difficulty of the conducting profession. It is roughly comparable to the nightmarish vision of a pianist forced to do all his practicing on a silent keyboard and having no access to an instrument producing sounds until one week before his recital! However, it seems to me that the disparity between classroom study and practical work in conducting need not exist to the extent that is commonly found, and that a better knowledge of the post-technical problems (which are mostly psychological) could save the aspiring conductor a great many agonies and humiliations, not to mention the benefits which the musicians could derive from it.

It is hard to understand why even some highly competent teachers of conducting have a tendency to neglect the psychological aspects. Perhaps it is because once a conductor has established his authority with orchestras, the psychological relationship with the musicians is no longer a problem to him, and he tends to forget what a fearful problem it may be to someone less experienced. Therefore I believe it is time that some of these problems be analyzed, and that some solutions be found. I am fully aware that it is beyond my capacity to supply *all* the answers, but at least I can begin the investigation and try to supply *some* answers.

The second reason that seems to justify my writing this opus is that in several decades of a conducting career that has never bordered on the stellar but has on many occasions put me at the helm of highly respected professional organizations here and in Europe, I have gathered experiences and made observations that may well be of interest to readers in the conducting profession and outside of it. Particularly during my early years in professional opera work I was fortunate enough to be in close contact with many outstanding personalities in our field. What they said to me, and to others in my presence, may be not only highly relevant to the matter at hand, but also hard to come by from other sources of information.

The main purpose of the book is therefore to investigate the various psychological processes that surround the mystery of conducting, processes in the mind of the conductor himself, of the musicians and, in a more remote sense, of audience and critics. The material to be dealt with is both intangible and elusive. But I feel that a beginning must be made. Once this has been done, many others may feel driven toward shedding light upon the problems in their own fashion. Conducting is so complex an occupation that even the most talented and experienced are not safe from making mistakes. Some of these mistakes could be avoided by carefully coordinated thinking and planning. Perhaps the analysis of some of my own past mistakes may serve to be helpful in that direction.

In order to enlarge the scope of this study and to supplement my own opinions by the most viable thoughts of a few outstanding authorities in the field, I have consulted ten very prominent conductors of America's leading symphony orchestras. Their contributions came in the shape of interviews that were granted most graciously. I have devoted an entire section of the book to these interviews and credited the opinions fully wherever they appear. If the writing thus ceases to be my exclusive spiritual property, the reader may feel inclined to pardon it since in this fashion some original and profound thoughts will be communicated to him which otherwise might remain inaccessible.

Since this is not a textbook, the question arises as to which potential group of readers should be most interested in its message. I feel that it is chiefly addressed to various types of conductors — particularly young ones — whose position and experience may not as yet match their artistic ambitions, and also to many musicians in professional and semiprofessional orchestras. Beyond that it is my hope that large groups of amateur musicians and untrained music lovers, perhaps at the cost of having to skip over some more technical points, will find enjoyment in it.

Peter Paul Fuchs
San Francisco, California
August 12, 1967.

Acknowledgments

Summing up the various sources that were helpful in the writing of this book, it is obvious that my biggest debt of gratitude is owed to my employer, Louisiana State University, for granting me a year's sabbatical leave, and also for providing me with an additional research grant, both of which were necessary in order to finish the book within a reasonable period of time. Particular thanks in this should go to Dr. Cecil G. Taylor, Chancellor, Dr. Max Goodrich, Dean of the Graduate School, and Dr. Everett Timm, Dean of Music.

Since the material contained in this writing has been collected over many years, it would be next to impossible to name all the individuals who in one way or another have made helpful suggestions or supplied necessary information. However, I should like to mention three men who have offered thoughts of more than passing value: Professor Tibor Kozma of Indiana University for his ideas on wording the Ten Questions; Dr. Eugene Zador of Los Angeles, California for various observations and anecdotes, Mr. Godfrey Layefsky, principal violist of the Pittsburgh Symphony, for his illuminating views on the orchestra musician's viewpoint.

Naturally, my warmest thanks are also extended to the ten prominent conductors who generously took time out of their busy schedules to discuss their views with me, and whose ideas are quoted in great detail in Part Three of this book.

And last but far from least, I feel most indebted to Dr. Bruce Howden, MCA Music editor, whose tireless efforts and expert suggestions helped immeasurably in the process of putting the manuscript in its final shape.

—Peter Paul Fuchs
Baton Rouge, Louisiana

THE PSYCHOLOGY OF CONDUCTING

CONTENTS

PART I

EXPERIENCES AND OBSERVATIONS.

Chapter 1.

The Conductor in Action — Magic or Workmanship?

The place is Carnegie Hall. An expectant crowd is filling the auditorium almost to capacity. On the stage about one hundred musicians of one of the nation's foremost orchestras are seated, tuning their instruments and warming up for the concert. The low volume of subdued conversation pervades the hall, mixed with the rhythm of steps and the rustling of clothes caused by some last minute arrivals trying to get to their seats. The general atmosphere is clearly fraught with the awareness of an important event that is about to take place within minutes.

Then the lights are lowered. The tuning on stage subsides, so does the conversation in the audience. The spectators' eyes become automatically focused on a small door to the left of the stage, where seconds later a short but sinewy man in an impeccably tailored dress suit appears. In his right hand he holds a short wooden stick, and he proceeds with energetic steps toward the raised podium in the center of the stage. Having reached the elevation, he acknowledges the thunderous applause from the audience with a self-assured smile and a short, graceful bow. Then he turns around to face the orchestra and waits a few seconds while the men and women on the stage ready their instruments for playing. After a brief preparation, the little stick in his right hand darts up in the air. When it comes down again in a sharp gesture that resembles the cracking of a whip, a majestic chord produced by a hundred instruments fills the great hall with a flood of overpowering sonority: the concert has begun.

This shockingly trivial description which, perhaps slightly modified, can be found in any number of third-rate novels, still pictures fairly accurately the sensations experienced by the average concertgoer at the start of a major symphony concert. We may easily dispense with the pompous literary embellishments, but after that we may well find it worth while to investigate the psychological situation that remains.

Without any doubt the man with the little stick in his hand is the focal point of the entire experience. You do not go to Carnegie Hall (or Philharmonic Hall, or the Academy of Music in Philadelphia) to hear Beethoven's "Eroica" but to hear (and probably see!) Karajan conduct the "Eroica," not to hear Tchaikovsky's Fifth but to hear it conducted by Ormandy, not to hear Ives but to hear Bernstein conduct Ives. This in itself may not be anything unusual: you also go to hear Rubinstein play Chopin, to hear Stern perform the Beethoven Concerto, or to hear Sutherland sing Lucia. But there is a difference: at least Rubinstein touches the keys of the piano with his own fingers, Stern handles the famous Guarnerius all by himself, and Sutherland has nothing but her own larynx to produce the legendary trills and coloratura passages. Yet the conductor

3

merely stands there waving a magic wand while others produce the music — others who toil with great abandon to create ravishing sounds anonymously, with little hope for personal fame or even credit. They make the music, and the man whose name you know so well and whom you have come to admire remains silent throughout the performance.

Naturally, even an intelligent child will protest that he controls the music, that all these musicians are the instruments of his will, that it is by means of their playing that he transmits his interpretation to the audience. On the other hand, if his role in the music-making is such an indirect one, as it were, why is he so surrounded with glamor? Why are the musicians in the orchestra not even allowed to acknowledge the applause until he, their leader, asks them to stand up? Why will even the least erudite music lover inform you that he bought his ticket for the sake of the conductor? And when he says so, is he merely following a convention, or does he actually notice the difference between Karajan's conducting and that of Maestro Johannes Suppenknödel?

Of the last we cannot be sure. But let us assume, for the sake of argument, that our faithful but not very well informed subscriber in the fifteenth row actually does possess a certain sensitivity that enables him to appreciate the presence of an outstanding conductor. It might be hard for him to prove this when listening to a symphonic recording or to the radio since even trained musicians are far from infallible under such circumstances. But in the concert hall he has no doubt: great music sounds even greater when conducted by a first-rate man, and *this* Beethoven feels more Beethovenish than ever before. Of course it helps to know that the man on the podium is internationally famous and to have read the glowing newspaper reports of his past accomplishments. But now we are moving away from the problem: the fact that there is a certain amount of pretense and even hypocrisy present in the evaluation of musical events is of little importance in our investigation. It does not even matter very greatly that some members of the fair sex will attend symphonic events primarily for the joy of displaying their latest fashions. What *does* matter is that in spite of all the lures of other events, there are still a great many people in our midst (fortunately!) who are willing to spend substantial amounts of money for the pleasure of attending live symphony concerts, and that many of them will freely inform you that at least in the absence of a name soloist their chief interest lies in the conductor, that to them the conductor's personality spells the difference between an exciting and a boring presentation.

At this juncture we may as well admit it: not only the conductor's work but many other elements of a concert can be enjoyed visually as well as aurally. This is at least one of the reasons why an ever growing supply of the finest hi-fi recordings has not managed to empty our concert halls. No "canned" rendition can ever duplicate the experience of being in the hall where the music is made, where the eyes may assist the ears in providing full enjoyment. And to concede that the awareness of visual stimuli is apt to add to the total sensation can hardly be termed shallow. In a symphony concert there is always a great deal to see: merely think of the view of a hundred musicians in evening clothes seated in a carefully devised geometrical arrangement on a festively lighted stage! There are the shiny bells of the brass instruments, the necks of the double basses forming a wall, the timpanist majestically presiding over his kettledrums lined up in a semicircle. And once the music starts, does it not appeal to one's esthetic sense to see so many violin bows perform rhythmical movements in absolute unison — a visualization of discipline?

Yet more impressive than all this is the commanding figure of the conductor in the center, a man who with a few relatively simple movements seems to create all this sound; who increases or decreases its intensity seemingly at will; who can make the music roar or whisper, weep or lilt; who can even with one imperious gesture bring it all to a sudden stop. This obviously is intriguing — intriguing in the same way as the activities of a jet pilot who, with a few well planned manipulations of the levers and buttons on his instrument panel, makes the huge craft come in for a smooth landing. What impresses us in either case is the striking manifestation of authority by which one man controls an apparatus many times his own size.

Admiring a conductor's work on the concert podium thus appears to us as a kind of hero worship which on a primitive level is based much less on the beauty of the music produced by a conductor than on the discipline which he exacts from his orchestra. To his guileless admirers he may evoke the aura of a military commander whose orders are promptly and unquestioningly carried out by the troops: a Caesar or Napoleon before whose iron will weaker men must tremble! Perhaps it is significant that the most fanatically glorified conductors are often those who by accident or design seem to dramatize their complete control over the orchestra; for example, Toscanini, Weingartner and Koussevitzky in the past, Stokowski and Karajan in our own days. The impact of a Walter or a Monteux had to spring from subtler sources. This is not intended to be an artistic evaluation one way or the other but merely an acknowledgment of the fact that the crowd sees the conductor as a leader first of all. The more he appears to *lead*, the greater his impression on the masses of concertgoers.

Perhaps we ought to pause for a moment to analyze this impression of leadership to which audiences seem to be so sensitive. Naturally a great deal of it is visual: an erect stance, secure and disciplined gestures, and an attitude of confidence. Contrariwise, if a conductor shows poor posture, wears a worried look, and obviously struggles to coordinate the various elements, even an unsophisticated audience will immediately feel that there is something amiss between him and the orchestra, and his capability to lead the musicians will be questioned. However, if this sounds like a bit of foolproof advice to all conductors — simply stand straight, make sweeping gestures and exude confidence, and everything will be fine — then I shall have to elaborate a little further. In most if not all cases the obviously confident attitude of a conductor is not the result of telling himself before the concert to *look* confident but of a technical mastery in the control of the orchestra that gives him every reason to *be* confident! If

5

this could be faked, then conducting would be very easy indeed! On occasion there may be a charlatan who, fully aware of his technical inadequacy, will train himself in front of a mirror to look like the great magician that is likely to overwhelm the more naïve members of the audience. Alas, his chances of success are slim! The fact that there is a large discrepancy between the leader's imperious gestures and the ragged, undisciplined playing of the orchestra will soon become apparent even to the uninitiated, and after a brief stretch he will emerge as the charlatan that he is.

Psychologically, whether we like it or not, the conductor's success depends on the visual contact with his audience. If suddenly all symphonic playing except the making of records were abolished, we would experience an incredible downgrading of the entire conducting profession. Hero worship in the customary sense would rapidly come to an end, and the most likely survivors would be specialists, such as the late Hermann Scherchen, who through his incredibly skillful handling of Baroque and contemporary music was able to gather a large congregation of fans on a mostly non-visual basis. Yet such a specialist would have to appeal to a special and rather erudite audience, not to the run-of-the-mill symphony subscribers. If this statement should need further proof, think of the many music lovers who will sit in spellbound attention when the Meistersinger-Prelude is played in a symphony concert but who will nervously fidget with their programs and listen no more than perfunctorily when they hear the same piece at the opera. Obviously the circumstance that in the opera house the conductor is only seen from most seats as a head-and-shoulder silhouette, and the musicians are not seen at all, takes a severe toll in audience contact. The crux of the matter is that to the average person buying a concert ticket the conductor is less the conveyor of a musical message and more the glamorous magician who provides positive esthetic enjoyment by the way he projects his authority and forces the musicians to follow the dictates of his baton.

I do not mean to imply that the average listener is indifferent to the music itself. When he tells you that he loves Beethoven's Sixth or Brahms' Fourth, he means it in complete sincerity. In all likelihood he may also be sensitive to certain purely auditory effects of the conductor's work, such as an unusually warm sound in the strings or a very exciting crescendo at the end of a movement. I am merely saying, again with reference to the majority and excluding a small elite, that the particular interpretative merit of one conductor's work as compared with another may be lost on him. His direct evaluation of a conductor would therefore largely be based on what to the musician must seem to be a set of superficial standards.

If this is the way in which the popular image of a conductor is created, how does the man at the helm himself feel about the psychological foundations of his work and about his impact on the audience?

Ever since Felix Mendelssohn, conductors have intermittently been attacked as vain, shallow people who carefully rehearse their every movement in order to make sure that not even the slightest detail of their pantomime will escape the admiring eyes of the spectators. Naturally the ones best endowed physically have always been most vulnerable to attacks. A well cut dress suit or a gracefully rounded gesture are equally condemned as cheap devices of showmanship by the detractors. (These detractors may well be in the minority, but usually it is a rather vociferous one!) Bülow's goatee, Weingartner's sparkling diamond ring, Toscanini's long, heavy baton ("a Turkish saber"), all were branded at one time or another as paraphernalia to impress the audience. Even Gustav Mahler, according to all reports an anti-glamorous type if there ever was one, could not entirely escape the accusation of being vain, and some Viennese even claimed that his limping gait, the residue of a childhood disease, was nothing but an affectation! And when Stokowski, a natural target, for reasons of his good looks and his beautiful hands, not only did away with the baton but even had the audacity to appear in films, his reputation with the purists was ruined forever. And so it goes: whether here or in Europe, some conductor will always be singled out as a superficial showman to whom a photograph taken from the right angle means a great deal more than all the symphonies by Beethoven and Brahms.

What do the conductors themselves have to offer in their defense? I discussed the problems of gestures, at least tangentially, with a number of leading men in the field. Their reactions were completely unanimous. Whenever this spectre — not by direct question of course, but merely by gentle insinuation — appeared on the horizon, the result was an emphatic, even passionate denial that there could be any connection between the planning of a gesture and its effect on the audience. One prominent conductor even went so far as to resort to obscenity in order to make his feelings on the subject abundantly clear. According to every statement given to me, and most predictably, there can be only one justification for a gesture: the musical reaction that it elicits from the orchestra. Of course this does not preclude the existence here and there of showmen conductors who are interested in the impression that their physical demeanor makes on the audience. However, it would be hard if not impossible to find any of them now in the first rank of the profession, and even in the lower echelons they seem to be a vanishing species. In our days the prevalent approach to symphonic conducting seems to be a giving and demanding of the best possible craftsmanship, and beyond that an attempt to be completely honest in the musical interpretation of the works performed. Even the maestro who is of high caliber and entirely sincere in musical matters but not free from a tendency to reap additional profits by the visual magnetism of his personality (such as might have been the case with Bülow or Nikisch) is seen less and less nowadays.

The "showmanship syndrome" thus can no longer be considered a serious threat. Yet there is another idea often linked with symphonic conducting which undoubtedly hovers over a great many minds, although the conductors themselves seem to be relatively impervious to it: the idea of a "sense of power" felt by the man on the podium when he exerts his influence over so many musicians. "Exactly the opposite is true," says Erich Leinsdorf. "It is a feeling of close

7

collaboration, very much akin to what is experienced in the playing of chamber music." And Leonard Bernstein explains, "It is not at all that I command a hundred people to do my bidding. We are all doing the composer's bidding." Similarly, Josef Krips exhorts the musicians, "Don't feel that you have to give your best to *me*, give it to the composer!"

These three representative opinions may not cover the entire field, but I do think that they show a marked trend among present day conductors, at least in this country. It is no longer fashionable to be Svengali and beat the slaves into submission. (For one thing the "slaves" are generally too well paid to tolerate such treatment!) More likely a conductor will say to the orchestra, "We are here to do a job together, and we shall do it to the best of your ability and mine." This is an attitude which the musicians can understand and accept much better than any attempt at ruthless domination. If it sounds a trifle self-effacing, the maestro may still rest assured that he will receive the lion's share of the credit, provided that his work warrants it.

More about this will be said later. At the moment let it merely be stated that even the friendliest and most undictatorial of orchestra leaders may during performance project the image of being an iron-fisted czar simply because he leads a perfectly disciplined performance. And this is where the distinction must be made: no matter what the psychological approach may be, there is no first rate symphonic performance without the man at the helm being in complete control. Friendliness and close collaboration must never result in lack of discipline. The man who presides over a symphonic performance may be dubbed a magician or merely a fine craftsman, but in either case his will must be obeyed. As Leonard Bernstein, who takes great pains to be known as a non-authoritarian, states it so succinctly: "If there should be an argument over any detail of the interpretation, *I* am paid to win that argument. . ."

Chapter 2:

Can Conducting Be Taught?

All major music schools in the United States, and some minor ones, offer a variety of conducting courses within their regular curricula. Among the titles we find orchestral conducting, choral conducting and band conducting, and often these courses are divided into undergraduate and graduate varieties. Normally they are as standardized as courses in harmony or counterpoint: they follow an established curriculum and use established textbooks. The students who take them come from all kinds of backgrounds. Many of them show no serious desire to become conductors of any kind, but enroll because the subject seems an interesting one, and because one never knows when he might be called upon to lead a musical ensemble. The number of great masters of the baton thus produced is probably negligible, but then few graduating pianists or violinists will consider themselves the equals of a Rubinstein or a Stern. Most of the baton wielders will graduate with the secure knowledge that in four-four time the beat of two goes to the left, whereas in three-four time it goes to the right. Some of them may even know a little more, depending on the talent of the student and of the teacher.

This has not always been so. The idea that aspiring conductors can be taught individually or in classes is a comparatively new one. Why has it caused such a flurry of activity on academic soil in the few decades of its existence? Are we now aware of methods to train leaders of musical groups that our grandfathers did not know about? Has the arduous road to the podium suddenly become a well paved superhighway?

It seems only natural to seek the answers to these questions from some of the prominent men in the profession. The late Giorgio Polacco, one of the best known opera conductors of the so-called "golden age," told me more than once: "To teach conducting is nonsense. If a man has musical talent, has mastered the score and knows exactly what he wants from the performers, his hand will follow his intentions without difficulty." Sir John Barbirolli states that he will not accept students "because the certain something that makes musicians perform well for a conductor, even against their will, cannot be taught." Toscanini and Furtwängler are said to have expressed similar opinions, and I know of no one in the profession that would claim to have studied with either one of them.

Others thought differently. I myself was privileged to study with Felix Weingartner who taught conducting classes for a number of years, first in Basel, then in Vienna. And he was not alone. Many famous European conductors gave at least a small portion of their time to teaching, among them Franz Schalk, Clemens Krauss and Josef Krips in Vienna, Bruno Walter in Salzburg, Sir Henry Wood and Sir Adrian Boult in London, Phillippe Gaubert in Paris, Volkmar Andreae in Zürich, and Bernardino Molinari in Rome. In this country Serge Koussevitzky, Fritz Reiner and Pierre Monteux were responsible for training an entire generation of conductors.

If conducting cannot be taught, what were all these famous men doing? And, less glamorously, what is being done every day in the music schools of our colleges and universities? Are all the students of conducting taking un-courses in an un-subject? Or is the whole thing a gamble in which every student hopes that he might be the one with the divine gift, just as one might hope to hold the winning number in a lottery?

Polacco and Barbirolli notwithstanding, it simply does not make good sense to assume that so many good and even great minds should be wasting their time persistently and on a well planned basis. A Weingartner or a Monteux would not have attempted to teach something which he knew he could not teach. And yet, what about all these conductors rising to fame over night, by taking over a performance on short notice without any previous training or experience? Toscanini, of course, is the classical example, but many others could be mentioned. Why should one study conducting if it is possible to become a Toscanini without study?

The astonishing answer to this complex question seems to be that both sides are right, given an entirely different set of circumstances. There are a great many facets to conducting that can be taught even to students of very limited talent. And there are others which a select few will master instinctively, and which many others will never be able to learn, not even with the best possible instruction. An efficient timebeater is not necessarily a good conductor, and some marvelous conductors are not particularly efficient timebeaters. Weingartner (as I was lucky enough to witness) raised his baton in rehearsal before an orchestra of awestruck students and hypnotized them into playing Beethoven's Ninth in a fashion that would have been a credit to a first-rate professional organization. Strauss, without ever moving his left arm from his side and with barely visible gestures of his right hand, led a performance of Beethoven's Seventh that was perfection itself. Furtwängler, in spite of an all but unintelligible manual technique, could stir an orchestra into music-making of an exaltation that left everyone speechless, including the musicians themselves. Did all this happen because of the superior knowledge and experience of these men? Undoubtedly to some extent. But beyond that, and most essentially, it happened because they all possessed such large amounts of what Barbirolli calls the "certain something."

Even though it is a complex of instinctive and unteachable qualities that distinguishes a conductor of the first rank, it would be a dangerous fallacy to assume that such a conductor will start his career with all these attributes in evidence, like Pallas Athena emerging fully armed from the head of Zeus. For instance, I am convinced that when Toscanini conducted that legendary performance of *Aida* in Rio at the age of eighteen, no one then saw in him the future idol of three continents. My guess would be that the musicians smiled at each other, saying, "Arturo is a good boy. He has talent. They ought to let him conduct more often." Of course I am also convinced that if Toscanini made any mistakes that night, as he undoubtedly must have, he became aware of them immediately and did not repeat them in the next performance.

The point is simply that some extraordinarily gifted individuals are able to absorb in a few hours of intelligent observation what others can learn only in months or years of hard work under the guidance of a capable teacher. This does not mean that the latter group ought to be neglected. On the contrary, they are the ones who need to be helped! Yet even a phenomenally talented young man can profit by instruction, provided that the teacher is a Weingartner, a Monteux or a Koussevitzky . . .

It was Weingartner himself who, during a class period interrupted the instruction, obviously in a reflective mood. "You young people of today are lucky," he said. "You are getting some systematic training in the basic technique of conducting. The only conducting instruction I ever received was from an elderly piano teacher at the Leipzig Conservatory who tried to cover the whole area with one rule: Make your beat always round, gentlemen, then nothing can happen . . ." Even so, Weingartner was not at all convinced that his training could supply all the necessary answers. At the end of a year during which we had studied with him a large number of scores from the Classical and Romantic periods, and even two operas (*The Magic Flute* and *Die Meistersinger*), he once remarked, "It is all very well to study the classics as we are doing here. But then probably some of you will accept engagements as theatre conductors, and the first assignment of a silly little operetta will throw you in a turmoil. You will soon realize that the study of Beethoven's Ninth did not equip you to cope with technical problems of that kind . . ." In my own case these were prophetic words. About a year later I became aware that certain tempo transitions in musical comedies, or even the conducting of a simple waltz, would leave me panicstricken. And what was even more humiliating, the second conductor of the theatre that had hired me as an assistant (a man who had no technical training comparable with mine, and whose only real asset was his ten years of practical experience) was able to handle these same problems with great ease. The impact of this discovery gave me a new respect for the much despised word "routine."

In fact, during my early years in the theatre my exalted education as a conductor was challenged more than once. One day the same above-mentioned second conductor took me aside and said, with a somewhat condescending smile, "So you can conduct Beethoven's Ninth? That is fine. Now tell me, how do you beat the opening of the first scene of *Traviata*?"

Knowing the music very well from having coached it with solo singers and chorus I thought quickly and said, "In two."

"Oh no, in four," he replied with a triumphant grin. "If you did it in two you could never get the afterbeats of the trombones together." He was right. I have conducted the opening of *Traviata* many times since then, but never in two.

What happens when a young conductor embarks upon a career in the theatre without the benefit of technical training? This is a procedure that used to be almost standard within the realm of the German theatre, and one that may not even be too uncommon now. (Of course it must be understood that what we are concerned with here is training in the technique of conducting. There are many other subjects that must have been studied most assiduously before starting any kind of conducting career: the piano plus one or several other instruments, harmony, counterpoint, composition and orchestration. More about that later. A good basic knowledge of the repertoire, both symphonic and operatic, is also indispensable.) Presently the young fledgling who wishes to pursue a conducting career feels ready for his first professional position with a theatre, or to put it more accurately, for "on-the-job-training." He plays the piano well enough, he has also coached and accompanied singers, and he feels full of enthusiasm and an indomitable sense of his mission. Probably after an audition at the piano, which may have consisted of the playing of some difficult passages from the vocal scores of standard operas, he is hired by the theatre as coach or assistant conductor ("Korrepetitor," "répétiteur" or "maestro sostituto" are the terms used in Europe) and perhaps also as assistant chorus director. His main job is to train the solo singers in their roles. Soon he will be called upon to play the piano at musical ensemble rehearsals and also at stage rehearsals. In between he may train a section of the chorus and perhaps also accompany rehearsals of the ballet, the latter being a chore that is much detested due to its lack of musical challenge. The next step would be backstage work, such as the cueing of off-stage instruments, or even the conducting of an off-stage band or off-stage chorus. These assignments are often difficult and responsible and require a great deal of psychological security and initiative from the young fledgling. They may also subject him to outbursts of severe invective from the conductor in the pit if anything should go wrong.

To illustrate how demanding some of the assignments of backstage conducting are I should like to tell the following true story: during the early twenties, the Vienna State Opera was under the joint artistic direction of Richard Strauss and Franz Schalk. Both, of course, were eminent musicians and conductors but of sharply contrasting temperaments, a circumstance that led to the early resignation of Strauss.

One night during a performance of *Tristan und Isolde* which Schalk conducted, about a minute after the beginning of the third act, the stage manager stormed into Strauss' office in great excitement. "Maestro X has suddenly been taken ill," he gasped, "and now we have no one to conduct the English horn" (for the shepherd's tune off-stage).

"Calm down, my friend," Strauss said smilingly, "I shall conduct the English horn myself." He followed the much relieved stage manager, arriving just in time for the first downbeat. (Of course Schalk was in the pit all the time and unaware of the change.)

I shall skip over what happened next. But after the end of the performance Schalk came backstage ranting and raving: "Who was the incompetent fool that conducted the English horn tonight? Everything was wrong!"

In small theatres an assistant may often be asked to play a piano or celesta part in the orchestra, perhaps even to assist in the percussion department. These assignments are particularly coveted since they give him a good opportunity to observe the chief conductor at close range. If he is both ambitious and intelligent he will not only try to learn everything possible by observation, but also to establish close relations with his superiors. This is helpful because the asking of questions may yield a great deal of technical information, and because his own conducting ambitions may well be furthered in this manner. For it goes without saying that the young man's eyes are focused on the podium all the time, and the sooner he gets an opportunity to conduct, the better he will like it. If the chief conductor favors his young assistant, he may soon become his mentor, teacher and father confessor. He may even take advantage of the relationship by asking the assistant to carry his scores after him or by sending him out for coffee during intermission. Luckily, I never had to face such a situation during my assistant days. But I am told that in the building of some careers it became a contributive factor.

(My own first chief conductor, a man of great erudition, was in the habit of taking long walks at night after performances, and he often invited me to accompany him. On these walks our conversations would cover subjects from

12

Plato by way of Michelangelo to Alban Berg, and I remember them gratefully since they added a great deal to my musical and intellectual development.)

After some months or even years of smiling servitude, the great day arrives for the young maestro, and he is entrusted the conducting of a performance. In all likelihood it will not be *Meistersinger*. Probably it will be the nineteenth performance of an operetta or musical comedy. And, ironically, it will happen without the benefit of an orchestra rehearsal, a circumstance that many an experienced practitioner might shy away from. But again, keeping control of a well routined production is not the most taxing assignment. On this occasion the fledgling conductor may encounter a psychological situation that he will remember nostalgically in later years: everyone will wish him well, the performers on stage and in the pit will be especially alert, and should he make a mistake they will try their best to cover up for him. One of the senior conductors may sit in a box, scrutinizing the young man's behavior with an eagle eye and offering helpful suggestions afterwards. Members of the orchestra will also add their advice, merrily contradicting one another. If the whole thing went well, or at least relatively well, it will have accomplished its purpose: more performances to conduct and eventually a promotion to a conducting position.

This system of gradual development of a man's capabilities, of working one's way up the ladder, so to speak, has produced many first-rate and near first-rate careers. But it has also been responsible for the careers of many conscientious craftsmen — men perhaps not capable of major artistic accomplishments, but technically clean, musically secure and generally equipped to lead performances of better than acceptable standards. Thus, it seems to be a thoroughly workable system. It might be added that in our days, when conducting classes are no longer anything unusual, many of the young assistants may start their theatrical careers after a year or two of formal baton training, as I did myself. In that case they will probably feel better equipped and less nervous when the great opportunity offers itself.

However, although the above described system works very well in central Europe, it is not applicable to conditions in the United States, at least not at this time. To begin with, we do not have a sufficient number of opera companies. Many of the ones that we do have offer only short seasons, concentrated, high pressure affairs that are not conducive to the gradual development of conducting talent. And even the major companies do not have much to offer in this respect. Usually they are prestigious, carriage-trade organizations whose stakes are too high to offer opportunities to talented beginners. Therefore the gradual promotion system for conductors has never really taken roots in this country. There is little hope that it will until a number of medium-grade opera companies offering year-round seasons can be established.

What shall we do in the meantime? The demand for qualified conductors is steadily growing, and orchestra musicians have a right to be protected from the bungling experiments of ill-equipped beginners pretending to be professionals. Should we simply hope that most of the young men wanting to be conductors will possess Barbirolli's "certain something" which in the long run will lead their efforts towards success? With humble apologies to Sir John, and without trying for one moment to question the validity of his statement, I would suggest that we must offer more and better training by truly qualified teachers — not by academicians without practical experience who have memorized the first ten chapters of Max Rudolf's textbook. If we cannot produce a Toscanini, a Bruno Walter or a Barbirolli in this fashion, we need not be too self-conscious about that: even among second and third conductors in German theatres there are not too many that possess the "certain something" to any measurable degree. In spite of that, most of them are respected as competent practitioners of their profession. This type of competency that commands respect even though it may not produce flaming headlines is what we ought to develop through teaching.

We pay homage, and rightly so, to the great men in our profession for their topflight achievements. But in addition to these born aristocrats we also need a solid middle class, men who will never reach the top but who will save our standards from reaching the bottom. Whether this middle class is well-to-do and respectable or decrepit and impoverished depends on the quality of the training offered. Instruction cannot take the place of talent, but it can develop whatever talent there is. And if in some cases there is not enough talent to be developed, then it should be the teacher's prerogative to steer the student toward a different career before he becomes the butt of many cruel jokes.

What can we teach our "middle class" students? First of all a clear beat, something that most musicians are grateful for. We can train their sense of rhythm, particularly in the assymetrical patterns. We can help them develop their auditory ability to distinguish intervals and harmonies. We can then awaken their sense of style and sharpen their sensitivity for the spiritual values of music. And finally, we can introduce them to the technical requirements and idiosyncrasies of various orchestral instruments, and also of vocalists, and explain how to deal with them.

According to Josef Krips, "a conductor who has learned not to interfere with the playing of the orchestra is already a pretty good conductor." Perhaps something of this nature ought to be made the minimum standard for entering the profession. I believe it can be done. With this in mind it may not be too optimistic, notwithstanding the privileges of genius, to call conducting instruction a worth-while activity.

Chapter 3:

The Road to the Podium.

"Tell me, maestro, when did you decide to become a conductor?"

The range of answers to this question is astonishingly wide. A conductor's development is so unlike that of a pianist who at the age of five may have picked out a melody on the keyboard, and who knew right then and there that this was his instrument; or that of a violinist who had a quarter-size violin pressed into his little hands when he was four, and who has never spent a day without the fiddle since then. The conducting profession as such is not meant for a child prodigy, notwithstanding Lorin Maazel who conducted the NBC Symphony at the age of twelve, or in older history, Felix Mendelssohn, who is said to have conducted an oratorio of his own composition when he was only thirteen. A conducting career may start early, but it may also start at a fairly mature age, provided that the aspirant's musical qualifications have been firmly established. The person who decides to become a conductor is frequently not a student but a seasoned professional musician, and the decision may be brought about either by a gradually ripening desire or by a sudden lucky accident. Famous conductors who have emerged from the ranks of the orchestra are legion: Toscanini, Monteux, Ormandy, Barbirolli and Wallenstein are but a few of the names that immediately come to one's mind.

Parenthetically, I should like to take issue with a statement attributed to Gregor Piatigorsky, as quoted in Time magazine, to the effect that "virtually any mediocrity can rise to fame as a maestro," provided that he possesses certain extramusical virtues, and that "a man who has never conducted or studied conducting is capable of giving an acceptable performance, and on the spur of the moment." The implication seems to be that conducting is an easy, overrated activity. But in the same article Piatigorsky is also quoted as saying that he (one of the great cellists of his generation and thus certainly not a mediocrity) tried his hand at conducting a concert once, but the results apparently did not impel him to return to the podium. If we are to accept the first statement, what can possibly justify the second?

It really does not matter at what age the decision is made to choose the podium as a career. A conductor does not depend on the extreme amount of physical conditioning that is necessary to become an outstanding instrumentalist, a process that must be started very early in life if it is to be successful. My own love affair with the baton happened to start at the age of nine, and it was love at first sight. But I realize now that if I had made the decision six or seven years later, while going through the same curriculum of instrumental and theoretical studies, it would not have affected my development very greatly. Maazel (or Mendelssohn) notwithstanding, it is generally difficult if not impossible to diagnose conducting talent in a child. Therefore the young man who waits until his faculties have ripened, and until the confrontation with a live orchestra can tell him whether this is what he feels inclination and aptitude for, has sacrificed little or nothing.

One reason why I made my own decision so early, and why in Europe it is often made earlier than here, is the widely held conviction among central European musicians that in order to become a conductor one must join the musical staff of a theatre as an apprentice, presumably at the age of twenty or earlier. This may sound strange in a country where young people often do not even begin to study music in earnest until they enter college. But it is a fact of life in Europe, and it rules one's thinking. Compare this with the career of

Leonard Bernstein who told me that when he finished college, although he knew that he would spend his life in music, the thought of becoming a conductor had not as yet occurred to him! Many other late arrivals on the podium could be mentioned. But all this is secondary as long as the career once decided upon is pursued with the fullest intensity.

Since conductors may come from a variety of musical backgrounds, it is natural to ask what the advantages and disadvantages of each background are. I have already described the standard development that takes the European maestro up the rungs of the ladder by serving in various subordinate capacities within the framework of the musical theatre. For this type of career, pianistic ability is, of course, a must. Perhaps it is not necessary to be a concert pianist, but it would be hard to imagine how anyone not equipped with excellent technical fluency on the piano could negotiate such scores as *Meistersinger, Falstaff* or *Rosenkavalier,* let alone *Elektra* or *Wozzeck.* In such assignments the better pianist will not only be able to transmit his musical ideas with greater immediacy, but with his manual dexterity taken for granted he will also manage to concentrate more on helping the singers, which after all is his primary function. Obviously in the early stages of the preparation of an opera the piano is the center of things, and the conductor who does not feel at home on the keyboard is bound to suffer. Thus the poorly-equipped pianist in an opera company may find himself grounded before he has ever had a chance to spread his wings.

In this country I have on occasion heard of opera companies where the conductor, not being a sufficiently capable pianist himself, would have to do all his preparatory rehearsing with the help of an assistant at the piano. This is possible if the company can afford the luxury of supplying a skilled pianist for every single musical rehearsal, beginning from the very first confrontation between conductor and singers. Even then it is, in my opinion, a clumsy procedure. In the early rehearsals the conductor should be able to give all his time and energy to the indoctrination of the singers and not be forced to stop ever so often for the purpose of explaining his intentions to the piano-playing assistant. It is generally felt in the theatre that there is no more efficient way for the musical director to shape the interpretations of the singers than by guiding them from the piano. A master conductor of opera should also be a master coach. Anyone who has been fortunate enough, as I was, to observe a Walter, a Leinsdorf or a Krips at the piano rehearsing singers will readily understand the tremendous psychological advantage of this approach.*

But the advantages that the pianist-conductor enjoys over his non-piano-playing colleagues are not confined to the realm of opera. His thinking is generally more adapted to polyphony than that of a musician who only plays one voice at a time. Also, with some additional training he may put his manual dexterity to

---

* In the same vein Elisabeth Schwarzkopf was recently quoted in *Opera News* as saying that she was very fond of Karajan's recording of *Falstaff,* because it "reminds me of the days when Karajan had time to sit at the piano and rehearse the most intricate ensembles so that they sparkled like diamonds and moved with the unhurried accuracy of a Swiss watch."

excellent use by acquiring the ability to play orchestra scores at sight on the piano. This is a great help in the case of many contemporary scores, where even the most developed aural imagination may occasionally be in need of help by actual sounds. Of course the warning is often heard that playing a score on the piano may blunt one's sense of orchestral color — a rather negligible danger, unless score playing on the piano is practiced to excess. I sense a far more real danger in the fact that the pianist's ears are attuned to an instrument which lacks a true legato, and evil tongues may accuse the pianist-conductor of living by a staccato philosophy. This tendency can and should be corrected by exposure to as much string music as possible, particularly string quartet. If the pianist-conductor can spend some time acquiring basic proficiency on the violin, viola or cello, it will further his balanced outlook even more.

In spite of the obvious advantages it is not my intention to claim that a pianist's background for conducting is superior to all others. Since the string players in the orchestra represent the numerical majority, a conductor insensitive to their problems may find communication difficult. String players more than any other musicians expect specific instructions from the conductor. It will not do for him to say, "Gentlemen, make this passage a little lighter." There are fifteen different ways for a string player to make a passage lighter, and if he is not told which method to apply, each musician will apply his own, the result being confusion, unless a kind concertmaster intervenes with "off the string, middle." (Which is what the conductor should have said in the first place!) Naturally the instructions must not only be specific, they must also be practical. Seasoned string players will tell you with great relish about the conductor who asked for punta d'arco in a passage where such a bowing was a technical impossibility. I am reliably informed that the conductor's image with the musicians did not benefit from this instruction.

In an article a few years ago, Eugene Ormandy made the very interesting statement that he believed each conductor was in the habit of using the physiology and psychology of his major instrument while in front of the orchestra. Thus he, Ormandy, displayed the attitude of a violinist while conducting, Toscanini or Barbirolli that of a cellist, Walter or Bernstein that of a pianist, and perhaps Stokowski that of an organist. On the basis of this fascinating hypothesis, it stands to reason that a conducting string player's movements might resemble the drawing of a bow across the strings, while a pianist would be more inclined towards vertical gestures similar to those used in depressing the piano keys. This part of it may be purely external but not unimportant since it is very comfortable for a string player to follow movements which directly suggest the ones he is making with his bow. But the analogy goes much further. The violinist or cellist on the podium will probably show the greatest concern for a perfect legato and a warm, singing tone, whereas the pianist will tend more toward rhythmical precision and clear, incisive attacks and releases. There is, of course, merit in either method, and the greatest merit would be in combining the two. But as far as the larger number of string players is concerned, the first method will have the upper hand, and thereby the string player at the helm of an orchestra will establish a natural contact with the majority of his musicians, something which a pianist-conductor may only enjoy after years of striving for it!

One of the natural pitfalls of a string-playing conductor is his inclination to overemphasize melodic elements at the expense of harmony and counterpoint, thus depriving a symphonic score of its three-dimensional quality. Disturbing as this habit may be, a really talented musician who allows enough time for study will, in all likelihood, manage to overcome it in a short time. Of course, he shares this potential difficulty with orchestra leaders of woodwind- or brass-playing background, who are also accustomed to concentrating all their attention on one line of music at a time. In every such case the complexity of the material to be dealt with on the podium will present a tremendous challenge to the novice. His ability to cope with this challenge will be one of the determining factors in the decision whether to pursue or abandon the conducting career.

An unusual and often quite fascinating approach to the podium is that of the composer. In former days the composer conducting his own music used to be the butt of many jokes. He was depicted as an awkward, desperate man, wildly swinging his fists in order to obtain from the orchestra a sound that simply was not forthcoming. The few composers who were also highly skilled conductors, such as Mendelssohn, Berlioz, Wagner, Mahler and Strauss, obviously do not fit into this category. On the other hand there are stories galore about inspired musicians gifted with but little ability to communicate their inspiration. Anton Bruckner is said to have been so awe-inspired facing the Vienna Philharmonic that he obsequiously refused to give the first downbeat. Jules Massenet pleaded with the orchestra to "conduct me well." It is, of course, understandable that a desk-bound creator of music, to whom the score represents a spiritual reality projected on paper, would be utterly overwhelmed by a situation where he must physically control all the complex and possibly unpleasant details of its instrumental sound with no practical experience to fall back upon. He may soon feel that he has become the victim of a conspiracy when it is really only his own lack of technique that conspires against him.

In my student days I was told the story of a young and unknown Viennese composer who had been given the fantastic opportunity to have his new symphony played by one of the leading orchestras but who unaccountably had been asked to conduct the performance himself. The rehearsal was pandemonium. The musicians, who may not have been too enthused by the project to begin with, attempted valiantly to read the manuscript but with questionable results. After some measures the composer interrupted with the words "Gentlemen, *something is wrong!*" (Is there ever a surer way to elicit chuckles from the musicians?) Lacking the aptitude to be more specific, he then confined himself to such admonitions as "more fire, gentlemen" or "more pathos." Yet he persisted in interrupting every few measures and let it be known that he was quite dissatisfied, which only embittered the musicians.

Finally the permanent conductor of the orchestra, who had been listening patiently in the auditorium, made his way to the podium. With a paternal smile he put his hand on the composer's shoulder and said, "Professor, let them play the way they want to. If you tell them so much it will still get worse . . ."

In recent years the image of the composer conducting his own music seems to have radically changed for the better. Composers with no natural conducting ability have the good sense to resist the temptation of the baton. Others, with little or no technical training, have achieved amazing results by dint of their native talent. (I am particularly thinking of Stravinsky, Milhaud and Copland.) Paul Hindemith, who only started to conduct his own works when he was already world famous, apparently became so enamored of this activity that he later specialized in the conducting of Bruckner's symphonies. And, if the stories can be trusted, the spectacular conducting careers of Paul Kletzki, Jean Martinon and Stanislaw Skrowaczewski originated as afterthoughts to their appearances as composers conducting their own works.

Interesting as these examples may be, it still seems a good recommendation that anyone seriously interested in a conducting career ought not to wait for fate to make its demands but should acquire all the obtainable training while he is still young enough to do so. Of course the actual technique of leading an orchestra can be studied at any time between the ages of 18 and 26, or even later, but this should not induce any aspirant to the podium to neglect the many necessary preparations. For one thing, a major instrument is indispensable, not because it will give the pianist an opportunity to play a Mozart concerto and conduct it from the keyboard or because it will enable the violinist to lead a Handel concerto grosso while playing the first solo violin, rewarding as these activities may be. The reason is rather a psychological one: in order to demand from others technical perfection on their instruments, one should have become familiar with what it takes through one's own experience. It matters little what the instrument is; the struggle for virtuosity is always based on the same premises. But it must be experienced to be understood. A conductor attempting to drill his first violins in a virtuoso passage, but never having acquired technical proficiency on any instrument himself, would be vaguely reminiscent of a nun trying to give advice on sex.

In addition to the study of one or serveral instruments, at least one of them to a degree of virtuosity, a conductor should follow the same outline of training as a composer: thorough education in harmony, counterpoint, composition and orchestration are definitely required. Furthermore there is a number of most desirable subjects, such as score playing (beyond the ordinary score reading which is a part of orchestration), chamber music, orchestral playing, choral singing, and the study of Baroque music, with particular emphasis on figured bass. It is regrettable that many present-day musicians approach music of the early eighteenth century strictly as outsiders, depending on arrangements or realizations for their playing.

If there is to be any emphasis on opera or the musical theatre (and which conductor would want to exclude it from his career?), a number of other subjects will be required, such as accompanying, coaching and preparation of roles with singers, perhaps also some dramatic instruction and participation in an opera workshop. It is most important for a future conductor of opera to learn the subject from as many different angles as possible.

This leaves us with one remaining consideration: is it sufficient for a conductor to be properly prepared in all relevant musical subjects, or are there other matters that deserve attention? The answer will probably depend on your viewpoint. Undoubtedly some of the great conductors of the recent past were men whose education outside of music was extremely limited, a fact which some of them freely admitted. From my personal experience I could mention two or three whose only non-musical interests were the movies, cooking and women, not necessarily in that order! On the other hand there was Weingartner, equally at home in Hindu philosophy, Greek drama or Molière's comedies; Bruno Walter, whose most casual conversation was embroidered with quotes from Shakespeare, Goethe or Dostoyevsky; and there is Ansermet, whose knowledge of mathematics and physics seems to be truly phenomenal. Can their familiarity with non-musical matters be dismissed as something perhaps admirable yet unrelated to making music? When Walter conducted *Figaro*, it was obvious that he was inspired not only by Mozart but also by Beaumarchais. And when Furtwängler interpreted Beethoven's Ninth there could be no doubt that the "Ode to Joy" meant more to him than merely words set to music. It was Mahler who said that "the most important part of the music is not written in the score." This certain element which starts with style but is really far more than style — call it "Weltanschauung" — can hardly be done justice to by an interpreter who knows nothing beyond what can be expressed in strictly musical terms. Music is not generally written in ivory towers; it is one of the manifestations of the cultural climate of a certain age. Therefore, it helps the musician greatly to know the other manifestations. Some aspects of Mozart's music can be understood much better when you have seen paintings by Fragonard or the facade of the Petit Trianon. Wagner's work gains in clarity by knowing the philosophy of Schopenhauer, and a great deal of new light can be shed on the tonal language of Schoenberg and Anton Webern by reading Kafka's writings. And even a very superficial familiarity with psychoanalysis can be most helpful in the understanding of a number of operas, from Mozart's *Don Giovanni* to Berg's *Lulu*. In the light of these facts, can a conductor of serious ambition depend on purely musical knowledge, the way a mason depends on brick and mortar? If he is lucky, he may have been taught some of the essentials of cultural history in college. Just the same, he should never stop adding to his knowledge of art, literature, poetry, psychology and many related subjects.

The real difficulty for the young conductor comes when his formal training is over, and he has to find ways and means toward creating a professional career for himself. Since in this country the natural method of making the ascent by way of serving an apprenticeship in an opera house is practically nonexistent, a reasonable substitute must be found. An aspiring teacher of theory who has received his college degree may apply for a position teaching theory in a small college. A conductor who has finished his training as a rule cannot obtain a position conducting a small orchestra since conducting a small orchestra can be a very large responsibility for someone without practical experience. And where is he to get the experience except by conducting an orchestra? Caught in this dilemma, the intelligent candidate will realize that he may be a "master" in name, but that in reality his apprenticeship has just begun. If by some coincidence an independent conductorship is offered to him, he should have the moral fiber to turn it down and earn it first. Many a potential career has been ruined by the failure to distinguish between talent and ability. The young man who has made a good showing conducting the college orchestra in the Meistersinger-Prelude (after it had been carefully rehearsed by his teacher!) has no right to call himself a conductor. It will take many more such experiences before he knows enough to start on his own.

Then what is the answer? Most ideally, I think, a position as assistant conductor of a major orchestra, serving under a conductor who enjoys universal respect. Most likely this will be combined with playing in the orchestra, either in the string section, or as the orchestra's regular pianist. As a chief asset this will give the tyro daily exposure to a live orchestral sound. He will also have the continuous opportunity to watch his older colleague at work, and he will gradually take over some conducting functions for which he ought to be ready when they are offered. Of course not very many of these positions are available. The next best thing would be a college position with some conducting opportunities, but under the supervision of an experienced man. Even here the process of taking over major responsibilities will be gradual, perhaps even too gradual. Meanwhile one can study repertoire, work with singers and instrumentalists, and gain all kinds of knowledge that in the long run will be profitable.

Perhaps one of the main virtues that we ought to develop in our conducting students is patience. The story of Toscanini catapulting to fame overnight has wrought a great deal of damage in many young minds, and far too many of our aspiring maestri are stick-crazy. They cannot wait for the great moment of standing on the podium, hypnotizing the orchestra and keeping the audience spellbound, and they tend to minimize all the extremely important but somewhat unglamorous activities that lead up to this moment. As a result the profession is getting crowded with young men who display a flashy talent for the physical process of leading an orchestra, even in a contemporary work of complex rhythmical structure. But it is often a shiny roof resting on fragile pillars since far too little attention has been given to questions of style and musicianship. A maestro of this type may excel in the *Sacre*, or Boulez' *Le marteau sans maitre*, or Stockhausen's *Gruppen*, and then meet his Waterloo in Mozart's Symphony No. 29 in A Major! This fate is well deserved, for to him the art of conducting is "the art of what I can do with an orchestra" rather than the physical and spiritual ability to project the composer's intentions. "The trouble with many present-day

21

conductors is," according to William Steinberg, "that they are short of breath. They get caught up in a number of trifling details but are unable to plan a long, intense singing line."

It would be a rather weak rejoinder to state that some bright young men have reached the top in spite of these failings. They know themselves that the "Eroica" is foreign territory to them, notwithstanding their manual dexterity, and after a few exposures any intelligent audience knows it. It is true that even a superficial maestro who possesses basic musical talent will gradually deepen his artistry as indeed some of them have demonstrated. But why do this at the expense of fine orchestras and of audiences who deserve better? I see no reason why the subscribers of a first-rate symphonic organization ought to be subjected to the performance of a classical masterwork replete with interpretative mistakes which any qualified teacher of conducting in a college could have corrected. I am often reminded of the stories told about some of the great Renaissance painters. When a gifted and ambitious youngster wanting to become a painter would enter the master's employ as an apprentice, the first instruction given to him was usually: "Here, clean my brushes!" I submit that many a "flashy" conductor's artistry and musicianship would have benefited had he spent more time cleaning the master's brushes before being allowed to paint the Last Judgment . . .

The upshot is simply that it is not humiliating to be an apprentice, nor a journeyman for that matter. "Conducting is very difficult," says Richard Strauss, "and only a seventy-year-old conductor knows the real meaning of this dictum!" A twenty-year-old one certainly does not know it. But he might take the word of his older colleagues for it and give himself time to develop. Thus he may help his own career, which will need sustenance after the first flash of glory is past, and he will also help the profession as a whole to be staffed with mature artists rather than with fabulously precise human computers. By giving the gifted young man the opportunity to develop slowly and patiently we shall undoubtedly raise the overall standards. This may possibly result in some respectability without glamor, but in no case should it produce glamor without respectability.

INTERLUDE 1:
Two Common Controversies.

Every artist who performs before the public must face certain perennial arguments concerning his performance, arguments which he cannot win because they defy any kind of final solution. The best he can do is win the approval of the majority and reconcile the dissenting minority as gracefully as possible.

In Mozart's *Don Giovanni* there is the final sextet, which is sometimes sung, sometimes omitted. If it is sung, you will afterwards hear some patrons argue, "Why did they have to do the sextet? It would have been so much better to end with the Don's disappearance." If however the sextet is omitted, you will hear other voices, just as loudly arguing: "What happened to the sextet? Have these producers never heard that the opera does *not* end with the Don's disappearance?" In Verdi's *Aida*, the final high B♭ of the tenor's aria is marked pianissimo by the composer. Traditionally, and for practical reasons that cannot easily be ignored, it is often sung fortissimo. In the latter case you will hear the enraged voices of the purists, wanting to know if the silly tenor had never noticed the pianissimo mark at the end of the aria. In the opposite case others will want to know why the stupid tenor could not have sung the end of the aria the way it is traditionally done, instead of almost choking on a pianissimo high note.

The conducting profession as such is beset by two oversized controversies which seemingly can never be silenced: should the conductor use a baton or conduct with his bare hands, and should he conduct with the printed score in front of him or from memory, without the help of a score?

The first of the two controversies is probably the one that engages more violent passions in the defenders of each viewpoint. This proves conclusively that conducting a concert is a partially visual activity, for if it were not, why all the excitement among the listeners about the presence or absence of a little stick? Basically, this is a matter to be decided between the conductor and the orchestra, and the audience's involvement is a vicarious one. For if the conductor's gestures are such that the musicians can derive from them all the information necessary to lead them toward their best playing efforts, what does it matter whether or not a baton is used? Obviously even the best-trained of listeners could not tell the difference with his eyes closed. So why all the noise, one might ask.

The fact is, however, that this has become an issue with our audiences, and through their participation the controversy has become more violent among conductors themselves. For that reason it deserves a few comments.

Historically, of course, the method of conducting with the baton is much older, at least among orchestral conductors.* It is said to have been used first by Louis Spohr in 1820, and ever since then most of the famous conductors in the field of symphony and opera have been associated with the baton method. Batonless conducting of an orchestra was first seen in central Europe in the beginning of this century when it was practiced by a Russian conductor named Vassily Ilyich Safonov, who caused quite a stir with this innovation. It did not find too many imitators at first, but over the years a number of illustrious names have been identified with batonless conducting, among them Stokowski, Scherchen, Ormandy (for some time), Mitropoulos and Bernstein. I do not know of any passionate pleas set forth in writing by the proponents of either method, but privately some of them have expressed themselves quite unequivocally in favor of one approach or the other.

First of all, I think it would be wrong and ungenerous to condemn either method completely, unless it had failed to produce results acceptable by general

---

* As is common knowledge, the vast majority of our choral conductors work without a baton. However, the conditions of choral conducting are so radically different that I do not believe it necessary nor helpful to discuss their motivations within the framework of this study.

standards. Certainly this does not apply in either case. I have witnessed many great symphonic performances that were conducted with a baton, and many others, equally great, that were led without it. For that reason, although my own personal taste definitely favors the baton method, I do not feel justified in opposing the batonless method on doctrinal grounds.

The argument most frequently advanced in favor of the baton is the possibility of achieving greater clarity of gesture. This is particularly true when great distances between the conductor and some of the performers are involved, such as in opera, or in large-scale choral works. As Bruno Walter puts it, "The more distantly posted musicians or singers will not be able to follow the movement of an empty hand with any certainty." This was perhaps borne out by the example of Mitropoulos, who, using no stick, seemed to have easy control of a symphony orchestra but was accused of visual ambiguity, particularly in the matter of choral attacks, when he conducted operas.

Eugene Ormandy, who used to be one of the most celebrated proponents of the no-baton method changed to using a stick a few years ago. When he was asked why, he replied that his physician had assured him the little stick would add at least five years to his life. This is easily understandable. The baton, when properly used, provides additional leverage for the arm. A movement that originates at the wrist — this would include everything that Rudolf calls "light staccato" — can only be seen by observing the short expanse of the hand from wrist to fingertips when no baton is used. To this the baton adds a length of between 16 and 24 inches of visibility, obviously a great help to the performers. Furthermore, since through every additional inch of baton the arc of the movement is enlarged, the conductor who uses the baton can afford to keep the radius of his wrist motions much smaller and thereby save a great deal of energy. It can also be said that the batonless conductor, realizing that the space between wrist and fingertips does not offer a great deal of visibility, may be discouraged from using his wrist and let most of his gestures originate at the elbow or the shoulder. Aside from the fatiguing effect that such technique is bound to have, it is also esthetically unsatisfying to see the entire arm move most of the time, since it allows for so little physical contrast. In turn, the monochromatic visual impression of the conductor's gestures is very likely to reduce the amount of contrast and color in the orchestral playing. Naturally this is a difficulty which a master technician can overcome. But it does point up the fallacy of the often-heard statement that it is easier to conduct without a baton than with it. Certainly this is not so when the performing body is an orchestra, and the greatest resources in color and expressiveness are demanded from the conductor's gestures.

Brock McElheran, in his excellent study "Conducting Technique for Beginners and Professionals," claims that it is easier to produce a smooth legato beat with the hand than with the baton. This I cannot agree with. I believe that if a conductor uses the size and weight of baton that is right for him — something that may require a great deal of experimenting — and if he has trained himself to use it properly, there is no reason why the roundness and smoothness of the

24

beat should suffer. The real trouble is — and this cannot be sufficiently emphasized — that many conductors of limited technical skill use a baton but move the hand in such a fashion as if there were no baton in it. They forget the basic tenet of baton conducting: that the focus of attention is the tip of the baton and not the tip of the index finger. As a result, the baton, instead of being the farthest outpost of expression in the body, flaps in the hand as a lifeless and meaningless piece of material. This, of course, is always bad, but you should not condemn the innocent little stick for the inadequate physical habits of the person using it!

Conducting with a baton, when properly practiced, is a highly sophisticated art. It has been refined and perfected by many master craftsmen during the past 150 years. This does not mean that it must be adopted by every orchestral conductor as the ultimate solution. But I do feel that every conducting student should at least thoroughly acquaint himself with this method. Having mastered it, he may decide that it is not for him and that he can express himself better without a stick. This we should respect. But I think that permitting the students to decide in favor of the batonless method without ever having tried the other would give rise to a great deal of physical dilettantism that we can ill afford to unleash on our orchestras. Perhaps the greatest virtue of the baton is that its correct use enforces a physical discipline that would be hard to learn otherwise. Let there be no mistake about it: the batonless conductor must be equipped with the same amount of physical discipline as his colleague with the baton if he deserves to be called a professional!

The other question, whether or not to use a score while conducting a performance, is an even more elusive one. It is well known that about a hundred years ago even concertizing instrumentalists used the printed music in performance, and that when Clara Schumann did the unheard of and played from memory, many critics resented it and accused her of being a cheap exhibitionist! Conductors did not start the practice until perhaps half a century later, and then they adopted it only very gradually.* Even today it has by no means become universally accepted, for if it had, there would be no need for further discussion. But it is practiced by the majority of symphonic conductors in this day and age, and many of them would no more conduct a symphony with a score in front of them than they would appear on the podium in an ill-fitting dress suit. The comparison is more than coincidental, for both procedures are largely governed by elements of fashion. The exception from scoreless conducting is of course made in the case of accompanying a soloist. Then the use of the score is accepted and carries no opprobrium.

One of my favorite stories dealing with this matter is the perhaps apocryphal one attributed to the late Hans Knappertsbusch, who allegedly once was asked why he always used the scores in his concerts. "You know," was his deadpan reply, "I am one of the last conductors that still know how to read an orchestra

---

* Interestingly enough even Bruno Walter states that although he always knew his scores from memory he did not start to conduct without them until quite late in his career!

score!" The tongue-in-cheek character of this statement is of course quite obvious, for the idea of anyone conducting a symphonic performance, no matter how incompetently, without being able to read an orchestra score is too fantastic even to be discussed. But if Knappertsbusch, the great non-conformist among conductors, indeed made this remark, then the jab at what to him must have seemed an attitude of superficial showmanship was undoubtedly intentional.

If the absence of a score in conducting symphonic works is considered by many to be merely an act of conformity with current fashion, then it is ironically significant how such a fashion can reverse itself on the spur of the moment. Not long ago I was greatly surprised to read a review of a New York concert given by the London Symphony under Istvan Kertesz in which the critic warmly praised the conductor's "courage" in unashamedly using a score and thus perhaps starting a new fashion! And I had naïvely been led to believe that such a procedure was neither courageous nor fashionable!

What are the *real* merits of the controversy? Perhaps one ought to start such an investigation by quoting the old saw, attributed to Hans von Bülow, that the conductor should have "the score in the head rather than the head in the score." Indeed, there is nothing more disconcerting than a maestro who, after conducting a few measures with a show of great passion, nervously puts his head down, seemingly having difficulties in finding his place on the printed page. Obviously no sense of form or musical cohesion can originate in such a performance where the conductor is giving his attention to the musicians only intermittently, between frantic attempts to regain his own orientation.

When Fritz Stiedry once conducted *Parsifal* at the Metropolitan Opera in a production in which I was responsible for the musical preparation, I asked him whether he knew the score from memory. (I knew that he always had the book on the stand when he conducted an opera.) "I may not know it completely from memory," he said, "but I always know what comes next." If this seems to be a rather elementary postulate, it is amazing how many seasoned practitioners of the baton will on occasion fail to live up to it. Know what comes next: this is basic! Whether the melody in the first oboe is doubled in the second clarinet only or also in the first bassoon is good and certainly important to know, but the absence of such knowledge will not necessarily lead to a catastrophe, nor will it interfere, other things being equal, with the formal cohesion of the performance. But to know whether the three-eight time starts after nine or ten four-four measures of identical rhythmical structure is a conditio sine qua non, and any attempt to cover up this type of uncertainty by faking will immediately be recognized even by a third-rate orchestra.

"Know what comes next!" The importance of this statement is something to fall back upon, in the face of many glamorous and often specious claims that are made concerning the unusual cerebral endowments of some of our better known virtuosi of the podium. Bülow, who according to all reports must have been a mental giant, is said to have made the statement that if by some ghastly catastrophe all documented knowledge of Beethoven's nine symphonies were lost, he could rewrite their orchestral scores from memory, "probably with complete accuracy." Bülow's undoubtedly honest claim was also a most remarkably unusual one. And yet, at the time when he said this he had in all probability conducted each one of Beethoven's symphonies many dozens of times. Just the same, anyone who is not aware of the enormity of such a potential accomplishment should try to write down from memory one single page of the score of any Beethoven symphony (preferably the one that he knows best) and I wager that he will not have to compare his own version with Beethoven's in order to become aware of the inadequacy of his memory! And as far as Bülow's claim is concerned, I doubt whether any living musician could match it with a clear conscience.

I am mentioning this because I have heard it said not only of Toscanini but also of some much lesser lights among conductors that they could write down from memory any score they conducted. Perhaps in the case of Toscanini this was often true although we have no way of ascertaining it. Possibly it was also true of Mitropoulos. But in many other cases I would consider the claim most irresponsible, and at the risk of endangering the glamor of some of our colleagues, I think it is time that the truth of the matter be faced with honesty. To be able to write down from memory the score of, say, *Le sacre du printemps* would be an achievement of truly legendary proportions. However, it would be as legendary as it would be unnecessary. A conductor can do a most workmanlike job of conducting a score from memory without being able to write down accurately every artificial harmonic in the second violins, or every thirty-second-note in a run of the third flute which is merely part of a coloristic effect. To be able to say whether, in a diminished seventh chord, F#-A-C-Eb, voiced in twelve wind instruments, the note of the third horn is C or Eb may be very gratifying to the conductor's ego, but it will hardly make a difference in the quality of his performance. Far be it from me to claim that in order to conduct a score from memory in a professional fashion it is sufficient to "know what comes next." At the same time it should be realized, even by the layman, that there is a vast gap between the ability to conduct a work without a score with complete mastery and selfassurance and the knowledge required to write it down from memory with any degree of accuracy. This is just a bald statement of fact, not an invitation to let laziness take over. For no conscientious conductor will ever feel that he knows a score well enough, even when the most seasoned musician in the orchestra could not detect anything amiss. The question in this case seems to be a practical one: is it really worth my while to memorize every single note in the second oboe part when an ever so slight compromise on the thoroughness of memorization would mean that I could learn three or four scores in the amount of time that it otherwise takes to learn one? My own answer is in the negative, but since this is a matter of conscience, every conductor will have to make the decision for himself.

Naturally, allowances will have to be made for the greater or lesser facility of a conductor in memorizing a score. If Toscanini at the age of eighteen, on a

27

moment's notice, conducted a performance of *Aida* from memory, this proves that his memory must have been fabulous by any standards, for it is unlikely that the young man who was not even engaged in a conductorial capacity should have spent many hours every day memorizing the orchestra score of the work. Mitropoulos was said to have known his scores so well that he had committed even the rehearsal numbers to memory! Other conductors may never be able to reach this state of memorization, and if they even approximate it, this will only be after untold hours of arduous labor. One maestro may have the gift of total recall, based on a photographic memory: he may conduct a work for the first time after an interval of ten years and only require one or two readings at home in order to remember every smallest detail in it. Another may conduct a score from memory and afterwards forget it so completely that he will not even recognize the music when he hears it played. (I am not suggesting that this is likely to happen to anyone in the case of a classical standard work!)

Furthermore, it should not be assumed that a conductor's facility in memorizing allows any conclusion as to his other qualities. It is a special gift which some possess and some do not. During my student days I often attended the concerts of a certain conductor in Vienna whose musical memory was the talk of the town. He could memorize absolutely anything with a minimum of effort. At one time, just having recuperated from a serious illness and still too weak to stand up, he conducted from memory the world premiere of a lengthy symphony of which he had received the score only five days prior to the performance! However, aside from his memory, there was nothing outstanding about him: his readings were unimaginative and pedestrian, and his easy and complete mastery of the scores failed to produce any kind of inspiration in either the orchestra or the audience. It was merely an admirable technical feat, perhaps comparable to tightrope walking.

To come to the essential point of this investigation: we shall find that on the most serious level of his art, the only one on which a conductor deserves our respect and admiration, the difference between conducting with or without a score is not as great as might be surmised. A conductor who wishes to maintain control over the performers at all times cannot afford to use the score in order to inform himself after every few measures "what comes next" in the piece. Essentially the contents of the music must be memorized, and the book should serve no other purpose than as a quick reference to details likely to slip away in the heat of battle, an occasional reminder, but never a source of new information. If this principle is properly adhered to, then the decision whether or not to use a score becomes merely one of personal inclination and psychological security. Of two conductors who may know the contents of a certain score equally well, one may feel that the presence of the printed information — "just in case" — will give him additional security in his task, whereas the other may be just as convinced that it will make him more secure not to be bothered with such external trifles as turning pages and that he would rather give his undivided attention to the performers. I happen to belong to the latter kind: in conducting a symphonic work it gives me more freedom to have neither a music stand nor a score in front of me. But I think it would be foolish for anyone who does not feel that way to force himself to conduct from memory, to take undue risks on the quality of his performance merely to do what he may think is expected of him by audience and critics.

And while we are speaking of the element of fashion, we might as well admit that conducting without a score has a tendency to be impressive. Critics often give it special mention, and if the work thus performed happens to be contemporary or otherwise quite difficult, the conductor who has memorized it may be almost sure, on the basis of this virtue alone, to be classified in a higher category than he might otherwise deserve. This may for the moment strike us as superficial, but it is not altogether silly. What influences the critic or spectator (for this is what he is, since in this case the eye matters more than the ear) is not a feeling of admiration for a man who must have done a great deal of homework. That consideration is secondary. It is rather the physical impression of a leader who stands up there in space, as it were, with nothing between him and the orchestra, giving his undivided attention to the musicians, with no mechanical necessities to detract him. Again we are in the sphere of the visual. Put the conductor behind an opaque screen and no one will be able to tell whether the score is there or not. But visual is not the same as superficial. Perhaps the appeal of the music does become greater when the conductor seems completely immersed in it. And since he does not stand behind an opaque screen, it will not hurt him to give a little tangential consideration to these matters. His purpose for being there is to control the situation, and without the need to resort to any showmanship he should *appear* to be in control. Therefore, even if he does decide to conduct symphonies using the score, he should use it as discreetly as possible, without calling attention to the action of turning pages. In short, he should avoid any mannerism that may cast a doubt on his being in full command.

What I have said up to this point concerns the conducting of purely orchestral scores, where every musician has the printed music in front of him. But there are at least three other aspects of the conductor's work that deserve attention: the conducting of oratorios and other choral works with orchestra, the work with instrumental or vocal soloists in concert, and the conducting of opera.

As for oratorios and choral works, I do not believe that a definite distinction from orchestral conducting needs to be drawn. Again, all read from the printed page, with the occasional exception of soloists in a cantata or an oratorio, but their assignments are usually limited in size. And the conducting of a chorus does not create an added difficulty as far as memorization is concerned. In fact, it is often less risky than that of an orchestra. I have witnessed situations where musically well prepared choristers would simply ignore a false entry given to them by a nervous conductor and would enter correctly on their own. And if anything needs to be said in favor of not using the score, it is the fact that choristers, even more than orchestral musicians, like to see the conductor's face once in a while.

Totally different is the situation in an instrumental concerto or vocal solo with orchestra. Here it is very unusual for a conductor not to use the score, for a variety of reasons. First of all, it is much harder for the conductor to memorize the average concerto than the average symphony. In a symphony he may find complex structures, but the interpretation is his own, and whatever happens in the playing of the work has been minutely organized according to *his* instructions in a number of rehearsals. Not so in a concerto. Here the soloist is the dominating party, and the conductor becomes the accompanist. If the soloist chooses to improvise ritardandi or accelerandi, the conductor must follow. This can be very difficult in the case of a rhythmically involved virtuoso passage on the solo instrument, even with the music on the conductor's stand. Without the score it is practically an impossibility, unless soloist and conductor have made music together many times and know each other well. Or unless — if this must be said — both soloist and conductor are willing to make sacrifices in the accuracy of the accompaniment. Besides that, the soloist always plays without the music, and if his memory should fail, the presence of an orchestra score could be very comforting in meeting the emergency. Luckily, these incidents do not occur very often. But when they do occur, the quick whispering of a rehearsal number by the conductor may save the situation.

Besides that, even if the conductor has taken the time to memorize every sixteenth- and thirty-second note of the soloist's part, he may have a hard time convincing the soloist that he really knows the music that well. And so it is usually considered the polite thing, and often also the practical one, to have the score on the stand. This is also artistically justifiable since in a concerto the cohesiveness of the interpretation only partially depends on the conductor, and an occasional glance at the score should not disturb it. If, however, it is completely counter to the conductor's convictions to look at the score during performance, then he may leave it turned to page one throughout the concerto, with no one being the wiser.*

While even the presence of one soloist performing from memory is likely to complicate the situation, it will be infinitely more complicated in an opera where an entire cast of solo singers and chorus not only perform their parts from memory but in addition to that can only give half of their attention to the music; the other half must go to acting. In this complex art form anything can happen, and it often does. For that reason it takes great courage for the conductor of an opera to do away with the score, but it is done on occasion. The difficulty of it will depend on the work being performed and on the amount of preparation that has gone into its production. *Fidelio*, which is a number of concerted pieces in fairly straight rhythmical patterns, with dialogues in between (a welcome rest for the conductor's brain!), is naturally more easily memorized than *Tristan*, with its three long and musically continuous acts, representing from the memori-

---

* The remarks made here about the work with instrumental soloists naturally apply also to vocal soloists, only to a somewhat lesser degree.

30

zation standpoint about the equivalent of three full-length symphonies. However, the so-called "symphonic" operas are not necessarily the hardest ones to conduct from memory. I for one believe that the greatest difficulty for the conductor arises where there is a great number of recitatives with complex orchestral accompaniment, such as in *Falstaff, Gianni Schicchi* or *Ariadne*. In such a case he should not attempt this feat unless every word and note of each recitative is clearly imprinted in his mind.

In every musical ensemble performance the amount of give and take that has been developed in a series of thorough rehearsals is of paramount importance. Nowhere is it more important than in opera. Here the conductor who has had the opportunity to familiarize the performers with all the details of his interpretation, but who in turn has familiarized himself with all their strengths and weaknesses, is at an infinite advantage. The pleasant by-product of such a rehearsing process is that the conductor has memorized the score practically by osmosis. Under these circumstances, and in a work of average difficulty, few conductors will give a great deal of attention to the book while leading the performance. It is much more helpful to keep one's eye on the stage where the guidance may be needed at any moment. Suddenly, the conductor may find at the end of Act III that the score is still turned to the opening of Act II. So much the better! But if she should suffer from a mental block that keeps him from remembering whether the orchestra has four or five empty bars during the opening line of the soprano's recitative, then he will know that the book is there to help him out.

One reason why operas are so rarely conducted without the score is that such an accomplishment is not likely to be given a great deal of credit. In concert, conducting from memory can be a "selling factor," but hardly ever in opera! Most opera houses are built in such a fashion that only spectators in certain locations in the balcony can tell whether or not the conductor uses a score. And — we might as well be blunt about it — the critics do not sit in the balcony! And as far as the performers on stage are concerned, they are busy with weightier matters. It was an eye opener to me, when I once conducted a performance of *Traviata* without the score, to mention it afterwards to the leading soprano, an unusually intelligent and sensitive performer, and to find that she had been completely unaware of it.

Summing it up, the essential choice in the matter is not one of fashion, whatever that fashion may be, but one of conscience. And for every musician the strongest dictate of his conscience should be to make good music. Whatever method favors this principle is the right one! In any case the decision is not "to memorize or not to memorize," but to conduct from memory *with* or *without* the use of a score.

Chapter 4:

How to Learn a Score.

When a conductor appears in front of the orchestra for the first time, at the initial rehearsal, he is of course expected to be fully prepared for his task. Nothing is more irritating to the informed spectator than an orchestra conductor who tries to assert authority over the orchestra but is obviously impeded in his efforts by his insufficient familiarity with the score he conducts. Perhaps he will be turning to the trombones when he should be giving a cue to the French horns; perhaps he will let a retard catch him by surprise; perhaps he will be giving an energetic downbeat, unaware that the score calls for a sudden pianissimo at that particular moment. It does not take very many such incidents to make him a laughing stock in the eyes of the orchestra. If he is in a position that enables him to hire and fire, the laughing will take place behind his back; if not, the musicians, throwing etiquette to the winds, may laugh in his face.

Laughing is a natural enough reaction, but it does not supply an answer. On a different level we must ask ourselves: why does this happen? Why does any conductor who is presumably intelligent and quite educated, incur the stigma of being laughed at or worse, when a few hours of additional preparation could have saved him from that fate?

To be sure, it is a very complex question. The course of action taken by the inadequately prepared conductor is a disastrous one, which for the moment cannot be explained by intelligent reasoning. Would you drive a car if you knew that one of its wheels was slipping off? Or would you even sit down on a chair if you knew that two of its legs were broken? But here a conductor, a man of talent and erudition, lays himself wide open to the most derogatory remarks which he could have avoided. Why?

As a rule it is not the "tenth-rate conductor," the man without any special talent or knowledge, who will come to a rehearsal poorly prepared. More likely it will be a musician of imagination, a man of established qualities, who will thus fail in one of his most elementary assignments. On occasion overwork may be held responsible to some extent but by no means always. There seem to be conductors who are always splendidly prepared for their rehearsals no matter how crowded their schedules, and there are others who may not be terribly busy but whose preparation is often noticeably incomplete.

A colleague of mine once made a remark to me which now, after many years, appears to be a great deal more significant than it did at the time when it was made. "I find it very difficult," he said, "simply to sit down and study an orchestra score. To study a score I must have a definite reason: I must know that I am going to conduct it on a given date in the near future." I can well imagine that this remark may be rather puzzling to the non-conductor. Yet I know very well what my colleague meant, for I have often felt the same way

32

about it. Preparing an orchestra score for the purpose of conducting it is an excruciatingly abstract procedure. You may read it, analyze it, memorize it, but essentially what you have accomplished in these silent labors does not come to life until the time when you actually confront the orchestra and hear the sounds. An instrumentalist in his practice has the immense advantage that whatever he studies is immediately translated into live sound, and all necessary corrections can be made immediately. The late Walter Gieseking once claimed that most of his practicing and memorizing was done away from the piano, merely by reading, and mostly during train or plane trips. Admirable as this may seem, it would be difficult for the majority of instrumentalists to imitate since it requires too much abstract thinking even for the musician of great talent and intellectual capacity. Yet the conductor who wishes to be properly prepared for his first rehearsal can *only* work in this completely abstract fashion. He cannot call an orchestra together and say, "Gentlemen, I am now learning Stravinsky's *Symphony in Three Movements*. Will you please play it while I learn it, so that I can immediately hear how it sounds." You will, of course, call such a supposition ridiculous, which it is. But is this not precisely what is practiced by some conductors (albeit without the above-mentioned speech), and yet they lack the courage to admit it to themselves? They feel frustrated by the too abstract process of learning, and so they merely go through a few perfunctory motions of preparation and do not really start learning the score until they stand before the orchestra, naturally with dire results.

There may also be other motives for a conductor's lack of preparation. They have to do with the mysterious drives of the subconscious — "the enemy within" — and are largely masochistic in nature. Since I can claim no professional knowledge in relation to this subject and since it is certainly beyond the boundaries of this study, I shall no more than mention it at this point, allowing the reader to draw his own conclusions.

But — to be strictly literal and rationalistic again — why is it sometimes so difficult to be prepared for a rehearsal when there is a definite objective in sight: a performance within a few days? I think the answer is that if the conductor's preparation starts at the time when he knows the date and program of the performance, and if he has never studied the programmed works before, then it is often already too late for adequate preparation. Sometimes you hear people say, "This conductor is doing a marvelous job of the Brahms Fourth — no wonder, he has conducted it dozens of times!" There is more to this statement than meets the eye. One might instinctively say, "what has that got to do with it? Why can't a conductor do a good job of conducting a work without having done it dozens of times?" Of course he can. At the same time it is undeniable that the man who has given public performances of a work before is at a definite advantage over the one who has not done so. He knows from his own experience that in a certain spot the strings must play piano rather than the mezzo forte marked in the score in order to make the theme in the oboe properly audible; that a precise speed is necessary to make a saltando passage in the first violins effective or even feasible;

33

that an almost unnoticeable retard is called for before the entrance of the trombones in order to enable them to enter pianissimo; and other details of the same nature. Of course, with growing maturity on the podium, it is possible to anticipate many of these technicalities without actually having experienced them in performance. Just the same, this type of experience is always helpful. A teacher of mine used to say, notably with a generous amount of pessimism, that "any idiot can conduct a work well if he has done it for forty years." This seemingly outrageous statement should not be brushed aside too quickly. Admittedly experience cannot make a genius out of a mediocrity, but it can at least create a certain aura of competence where otherwise there would be nothing.

But as far as preparedness for orchestra rehearsals is concerned, what is the answer? In my opinion, it is basically a certain amount of continuing preparation for all kinds of tasks. It may be true that it is difficult for a conductor to prepare himself unless there is a definite performance in sight, but he can maintain a steady stream of study of the important repertoire, a kind of daily dozen of the conducting profession. This may not solve all the necessary problems, but it will supply enough of a basis that once there is a definite objective, time will not be too short to put the finishing touches on the preparation. Thus the only hazardous task will be the sudden assignment of a new or unusual work. But with so much of the other preparation out of the way, the conductor should be able to give almost his entire energy to this task.

The procedure which I am suggesting may be an unusual one in terms of what is generally done, but it is certainly not unusual by comparison with the habits of other musicians. Can one possibly imagine a pianist or violinist who would start his practice two weeks before a concert? Then why should a conductor be different merely because the physical plays a lesser role in his work? Such a viewpoint must seem rather primitive and not at all in accord with the stringent demands of the present day symphonic repertoire. Of course there is no denying that the suggested regimen requires a great deal of mental discipline. But need one really apologize for expecting discipline from the most responsible practitioners of one of the most difficult and exalted musical occupations?

If a general and continuous process of studies is a definite requirement for the conductor, the most exacting and challenging part of the preparation is still the period immediately preceding the first rehearsal. This is when intimate and complete familiarity with the score must be accomplished. And here I think the manner of procedure is of the greatest importance. It is not sufficient to study the melodic, harmonic and rhythmical structure of the music and to absorb all the details of the orchestration. May I be forgiven if the following sounds redundant, but I feel that I have ample reason to say it: the primary thing that a conductor must understand about a composition is its formal structure, first in broad outlines, such as the introduction, exposition, development and recapitulation in a sonata form, and then down to the smallest details. By this I mean the phrase-by-phrase understanding of the contents, the exact counting of measures in each phrase and the disposition of leading voices, counterpoints and subsidiary voices (something which Schoenberg and his school very accommodatingly marked with special signs, but which in other scores will have to be found and analyzed by the conductor himself). Whether the conductor wishes to establish all these elements by pencil markings or merely remember them will depend on his kind of memory. I have found the pencil marking method very useful, particularly when it comes to the periodicity of the melodic and rhythmical line. I know that some of my colleagues shy away from this minute dissecting process, feeling that it is on the prosaic side and that it may dull their senses to the broad sweep of the music. This I think is unrealistic. We must master these details to the fullest, and their knowledge should no more interfere with the sense of the beauty of the music than it should impede a painter in his realization of the beauty of the human body that he is intimately familiar with the structure of its skeleton. Periodicity is the pulsebeat of the music, and only the conductor who has taught himself to think in terms of bar-units can render full justice to every structural detail, and to the rise and fall of its thematic sequence.

After this has been done, and after the melodic and rhythmical units of the composition have been studied and analyzed in great detail, the next process which is likely to absorb most of the conductor's time and energy is the harmonic analysis. The intricacy of this process will naturally depend on the style of the piece. In a Baroque or pre-classical composition it may follow outlines that are so well established as to eliminate all major problems. Beginning with Beethoven however the harmonic structure cannot be dealt with thoroughly enough. Think for instance of the marvelous transition from the scherzo to the finale in Beethoven's Fifth Symphony which starts on the sixth step of C Minor, almost in the character of an improvisation, and which very gradually and with the utmost logic advances toward the triumphant C Major which opens the last movement! Or think of the fascinating crescendo in the development section of Brahms' First, beginning with the pianissimo entrance of the contrabassoon! The langorous ambivalence of harmonies in the introduction of César Franck's Symphony in D Minor, the stirring harmonic jumps in the scherzo of Bruckner's Eighth, the tantalizing playfulness of harmony in the opening of Strauss' *Don Quixote*! In each of these examples only the complete understanding of the harmonic functions can enable the conductor to build the musical form convincingly.

It hardly needs to be stated that in the average contemporary work the understanding of the harmonic structure requires far more patience and inquisitiveness than in most of the Classical scores. Here again, too much is being taken for granted too often, resulting in many indifferent performances of works that deserve better. It is true that to many people in the audience the subtle harmonic tensions and relaxations of a Berg, a Henze or even a Bartók may only represent ugly and disagreeable sounds, no matter how well they are played. To many, but not to all! For that reason it is unforgivable for the conductor to be cynical in matters of contemporary harmony and texture, as many unfortunately are. The myth that the contemporary composer writes simply "dissonant" music, meaning that the sounds do not conform to a conventional harmonic pattern and that therefore it does not make too much difference how the vertical array of voices adds up acoustically is bad enough as a view held by a layman, but in the mind of a serious conductor there is no room for it whatever. No conductor can be forced to love every piece of contemporary music put before him (nor, for that matter, every piece of classical music). But if he is to perform a score, he must at least make every possible effort to uncover its inner drives — with harmonic elements surely put in a leading position — so that even a relatively poor work has a chance to present itself in the fashion intended by its composer.

As I have pointed out before, in the harmonic analysis of an orchestra score the ability to play scores at sight on the piano is extremely helpful, and it should be greatly recommended particularly in the preparation of contemporary works. It is true that the harmony reproduced on the piano gives little or no clue as to the orchestral texture or color of a sound combination. This is unfortunate, but it is no reason to discard the entire procedure. The vertical accumulation of a group of tones still has an absolute value as a harmony which does not change, be it played on the piano or by five saxophones and a guitar. As a point of departure this absolute value of the harmonic unit which can be clearly brought out on the piano is the conductor's indispensable stock in trade. Proceeding from there to the elements of texture and orchestral color, he will simply have to use his imagination. Only let it be said that his imagination in these matters will be of little use to him unless the harmonic picture has been clearly established from the very beginning.

By the time this part of the studying process is finished, the conductor, while reading the score, should be able to project a reasonably accurate picture of the actual orchestral sound in his mind. The difficulty of this will of course vary with the style and complexity of the work. In a Haydn symphony it should be possible practically at first sight and certainly without consulting the piano. On the other hand, in Henze's Fifth Symphony it may take a great deal of concerted effort. But in no case should it be entirely impossible. And in no case should the conductor take a chance on letting himself be surprised by the sound of the orchestra during the first rehearsal.

There is another device that may be very helpful in this procedure, provided that it is used with great discretion: the phonograph record or tape recording. Of course I think it would be completely wrong to start the study of a score by listening to a record or tape. We must consider this an unorthodox shortcut, for although it may save some effort in experiencing the orchestral sound, it will at the same time act as a mental straitjacket and predetermine the interpretation, with the result that the ensuing performance may be pedestrian and sterile. It is my conviction that in the process of gradually bringing the sound of a score to life in his mind, the conductor should simultaneously work out his interpretation in every detail. He should clearly plan the exact speed of each section, the exact amount and degree of ritardandi and accelerandi, the scale of dynamics, the arrangement of leading and subsidiary voices, and many other matters that will govern the reality of sound he is to create. When all this is clear in his mind he may listen to a recording, preferably one made by a conductor whom he respects and whose style of interpretation he finds congenial. Even so, he may not agree with everything he hears, but by this time his own ideas should be definite enough that they will remain intact even though the recording may contradict them. I do not mean to imply that the conductor must preserve his own interpretation in a harness of steel. Everyone makes small corrections in the process of preparing a work for performance, possibly even during the actual procedure of rehearsing the orchestra. However, the conductor who deserves respect, while allowing for a certain flexibility, should remain an interpreter and should not become an imitator.

There is still another use of recordings in the course of studying a score that is possibly of even greater importance: as an aid to memorization. Max Rudolf, in his *The Grammar of Conducting*, suggests that it is practical to memorize scores in this fashion, but he also warns against the danger of using a recording either as a shortcut in the slow study process, or as an interpretation-shaping factor. It should be remembered that even in the memorizing process the recording or tape should be used only in the final stages. Once a conductor has memorized a score through the ordinary process of repeated readings, committing it to memory in units of a few measures at a time, he will then gain a great deal of additional assurance by listening to the record a few times. This will not only establish a continuity that would be hard to establish by merely thinking it through, but will also call one's attention to spots where there is still an area of doubt, inviting further study of the printed page. Again, under no circumstances should the record or tape be consulted at a stage where the areas of doubt still outweigh the areas of certainty.

Summing up, it may be said that the conductor who is gifted with better than average mental faculties (and what conductor would admit that he is not!) will be able to study even a complicated orchestra score in a few days of arduous and concentrated labor in such a fashion that he may face the orchestra without undue fear. However, the main emphasis should rest on the fact that preparing scores for conducting is a continuous process, not a tour de force to be rushed into in order to assure the success of one impending performance. It has been said that a conductor should practice his craft daily by technical exercises in front of a mirror. Perhaps so. But I think that it is far more essential to exercise the brain by a regular regimen of study, analysis and memorization so that when the actual challenge of a performance arises, the mind will be able to respond quickly and in a disciplined and well coordinated fashion.

INTERLUDE 2:

The Keys on the Conductor's Piano, or What Makes the Musicians the Way They Are?

According to a story whose authenticity I cannot vouch for, Arthur Nikisch, was once asked why he was so rigidly authoritarian in his attitude toward orchestras. "Why should I be otherwise?" he replied. "When I play the piano, do I ask the keys how the music should sound?"

Nikisch has been dead for almost fifty years, and in the meantime many things have changed in the relationship between conductor and orchestra. No musician in any orchestra of consequence in our days would enjoy the idea of being compared to a piano key, and his financial and social position generally allow him to be a great deal more assertive than in Nikisch's days. Even Toscanini's famous outbursts of invective and name calling that happened much more recently will probably not be repeated by anyone in the foreseeable future. Today's musician is an opinionated, outspoken, sometimes vociferous human being. He is intelligent enough to know that in artistic matters the will of the leader must be obeyed. But he also realizes that this does not deprive him of the right to be respected as a human being.

The psychological problem confronting every conductor is that he is only one against so many, and that he must make the best of this disproportionate numerical arrangement. Sometimes, on the basis of his position and authority, he may put himself in clear opposition to the entire group and still emerge as the winner. But few conductors in our days enjoy working on such terms. Most of them would like to feel something in the relationship beyond respect or admiration. If it is not love, it should at least be friendliness and cordiality. For when the musicians are on the conductor's side, they will help him in every possible respect and fight many of his battles for him. But beware when they are not! "It is never safe to conduct an orchestra of enemies," Izler Solomon said to me. "They may officially obey your orders, but they can always find subtle ways of making you appear at your worst, no matter how good you are."

Orchestra musicians as a group are certainly no worse than any other group of human beings, in fact, probably better. For at the risk of seeming to sermonize, I must say that I believe in the character-improving properties of great music, especially through continuous exposure. If a musician were completely untouched by the adagio of Beethoven's Ninth, for instance, chances are that he would have changed his profession long ago. The men and women in a symphony orchestra generally like their calling, and they like it particularly well when a conductor spurs them on toward their finest efforts. In an orchestra musician's love of music there is only one qualifying factor — how severely qualifying depends on his position within the orchestra — namely, that at one time he may have envisaged a better future for himself. It is rare that a young man or woman pursues serious study of the violin with the ambition to become a second violinist in an orchestra. Such a position is usually a last resort, when everything else has failed, and perhaps only a temporary stopgap. The first and second violin sections of our major orchestras are populated with legions of players who at one time saw themselves as future Sterns or Francescattis. And this goes not only for violinists. Most musicians had aimed far higher before the orchestra swallowed them. This is perhaps lucky, for there is no real capability in one's work unless one has at one time given it every fiber of one's being. Show me an orchestra without frustrated musicians, and I will show you a bad orchestra.

It cannot be sufficiently stressed that the crux of the conductor's work is the contact with live human beings. They, like other human beings, have their likes and dislikes, their loves and hates, their good and bad habits. These the conductor must learn to understand, or his greatest talent and best efforts will come to naught. He may possess the finest technical equipment, the most phenomenal sense of interpretation, the most perfect ear, but if he cannot find a psychological bridge to the people who produce the sound for him, he is bound to fail.

How does one understand these hopes and fears, these passions and frustrations? A conductor who has been at the helm of the same orchestra for a number of years will probably have had enough personal contact with many of the individual players to anticipate their reactions reasonably well. But what does the newcomer do who barely knows the musicians' names and nothing at all about their personal lives?

He may be an amateur psychologist who can tell a great deal about a man by the way he looks at him or by the way he takes his instrument out of the case. If he does, it will give him a considerable advantage in his work. But if he does not, there is still a powerful clue that he may use: the instrument that each musician plays.

Perhaps the idea that a musician's instrument should be a driving force in the shaping of his character seems a bit far-fetched at first. But why should it be? A drill sergeant who barks orders all day long will of necessity be different in his behavior pattern from a bookkeeper who says little and keeps his mind concentrated on a set of figures. A musician, once he has reached the degree of proficiency that enables him to play in a professional orchestra, will have spent the better part of his waking hours practicing his instrument. This involves an extensive conditioning process, both physical and mental. Since this conditioning process differs with each instrument, it is only fair to allow for the shaping of different personalities. The physical tension of a cellist is far different from that of a timpanist, and the breath problems of a flute player have little or nothing in common with those of a trombonist. Beyond that, the psychological role of each instrument in the ranks of the modern symphony orchestra creates an even clearer distinction between musicians.

It would be shortsighted in the extreme for the conductor not to take advantage of these known facts, and of the conclusions that can be derived from them. He may not know how the background, the financial status or the love life of the first cellist differs from that of the tuba player. But he does know (or should know) the physical and mental problems that each of them encounters in the playing of his instrument, and this knowledge he should use to the fullest.

Since all this may be a precarious hypothesis, let us first attack it negatively. Who has ever known a timid, self-effacing trumpet player, a loud-mouthed, uncouth oboist, or a relaxed, happy-go-lucky French hornist? Naturally I am only referring here to seasoned professional personnel who have lived with their instruments for a long time, not to students or amateurs. Furthermore, I am not prepared to prove my contentions on a scientific basis nor to claim that they must apply in each and every case. Yet a theory that may turn out to be worthless in one out of ten cases may still be highly useful in the other nine.*

Perhaps a more general perspective of the problem will be helpful toward its further understanding. The two sources of energy in the human body that are used for the playing of all musical instruments are the musculature of the back, the shoulders, the arms and hands (and very occasionally the feet), and the breathing apparatus from lungs to lips. Principally this defines the difference between string and wind players. A string player needs an extreme amount of coordination and often great strength in his arm and hand muscles, but his breathing equipment is not called upon for anything beyond the normal requirements of living. The wind player, on the other hand, must develop a tremendous amount of strength and control in his breathing mechanism, while the tasks assigned to his arms and hands are, on the whole, of a minor nature. Since the wind player uses his breath to such an extent, a normal and healthy posture is always demanded from him. Not so the string player to whom a crouched, bent-over posture is second nature. The first thing that a beginner on the violin learns is how to support the instrument through pressure from shoulder and chin only, without the help of the hand, an action that makes a normal posture virtually impossible. Besides that, string players in symphonic works are far busier than wind players. They play many more notes, yet the effort needed to produce one individual note is usually much greater on a wind instrument.

These few simple facts already account for a great many peculiarities and idiosyncrasies. String players, due to their unnatural posture, tend strongly toward backaches. For instance, every seasoned conductor knows that the first ones in an orchestra to complain about uncomfortable chairs are always the cellists. Also, since string players have to read so many notes from a strained body position they are very likely to complain about bad lighting or about light shining in their eyes. Wind players, on the other hand, are far more susceptible to upper respiratory infections and their side symptoms since they interfere with breathing. A small fever blister which a violist would ignore can put a horn player out of commission for several days. Furthermore, wind players, and particularly wood-

---

* I should not be too surprised to learn that someone else may have expressed similar thoughts before. If this is the case, then I certainly apologize to the original father of the idea for this bit of unconscious plagiarism.

40

wind players, are extremely sensitive to changes in temperature. Their instruments are built to very precise specifications, and their pitch requirements can easily be thrown off balance through expansions or contractions of the material due to changing temperature. Thus, a clarinetist whose instrument is built for a temperature of 70° Fahrenheit may find it difficult or impossible to control the pitch when the temperature rises to 80°.

In addition to that, although the string players are more subject to general tiredness, nervousness and irritability, the wind players are more exposed to specific hazards, such as the acoustics of a hall or a changed seating arrangement. While a violin player will always be able to hear at least the other violins, which may be sufficient for sound orientation, a first trombonist playing in a new hall may suddenly be unable to hear the first horn part on which he had always depended for his own intonation and dynamics, causing him extreme insecurity and disorientation.

These are general problems, involving the entire body of strings or the entire choir of winds at a time. The problems that concern each individual instrument according to its playing characteristics and its typical function within the orchestra are far more serious, and also of far greater determinating force in shaping the musicians' characters. In order to realize some of the problems — not nearly all of them — it is sufficient to take the score of a well known classical work, say a Brahms symphony, and read one line at a time, making an attempt to put oneself into the psychological situation of the musician who plays that line. For instance: "suppose I am the first clarinetist. For the first thirty-six measures of this movement I have played a subsidiary voice in a loud tutti passage. If I did not play too many wrong notes or rhythms and if I did not conspicuously enter when I should have been silent, then I probably have remained unnoticed so far by the conductor and by my fellow musicians. Now suddenly my beautiful solo line approaches. I must modulate my tone from the comparative heaviness of the tutti to a gentle, soaring piano espressivo. I must sing the line, mold it, shape it with an expression of sublime beauty as if I had composed it myself. How do I feel about it? Am I nervous or relaxed? Do I feel that the conductor trusts me, or is he maliciously waiting for me to crack on a high note or to breathe in the wrong place? Do I know how to give him exactly what he wants, or can I perhaps even play the phrase so beautifully that it will surprise him? Let's try. Ah, he smiled. He seems to like it! Now I shall feel much better about the more difficult solo at the end of the movement! . . ."

The playing of a symphony consists of thousands of such individual thoughts, reactions and motivations. Do we as conductors realize this? Do we sufficiently sympathize with the problems of the individual musician?

Take, for instance, the first trumpet player. If the piece happens to be *Petrouchka*, or Strauss' *Heldenleben* or Shostakovich's First, he has many difficult and interesting solos and is constantly in the limelight. But what about symphonies by Haydn and Mozart and some by Beethoven, Schubert and Mendelssohn? Here he may have to play three notes, then count forty-eight measures of rest, play another five notes (always on alternating tonic and dominant) and count another fifty-six measures of rest. What he plays in this type of music is always quite audible, but it is rarely challenging or important (to him!). Small wonder that his intermittent assertiveness finds its way into his personal behavior. He is often heard to complain about something, and more often than not in a loud voice. He is the born spokesman for his colleagues, and noble restraint is not always his greatest virtue. On the other hand it is wrong for a conductor immediately to suspect evil or disrespectful motives behind the often conspicuous mannerisms of a trumpet player. The counting of rests can be a dreary business, and when a kindred spirit sits next to you who has just as many rests to count, the temptation to shorten the waiting time by telling a little joke may be hard to resist.

Generally speaking, musicians should not be condemned for their little idiosyncrasies unless they fail to enter at the proper time or cause serious infringements of the necessary discipline. If the timpanist, for instance, seems to be engrossed in the reading of a newspaper during a rehearsal, the conductor should not instinctively react with an angry reprimand. It may well be that he has nothing to play until the following movement, and if that contingency should have escaped the conductor's attention, then his reprimand might quickly backfire and cause him to lose the respect of the entire orchestra.

It is very important for the conductor to realize where his phychological troubles in the orchestra are most likely to originate. Delicate personalities are quite naturally the privilege of players of delicate instruments, and I would unhesitatingly put the oboe and the French horn at the top of this column. And quite naturally the first oboe and the first French horn, holding the most exposed positions within their instrument groups, are most likely to show signs of strain.

The typical oboe player would be tempermentally the exact opposite of the typical trumpet player: shy, nervous and a man of few words. Playing an instrument that is penetrating but not very loud, that must sing with lyrical beauty in spite of great problems inherent in its intonation and attack, he may seem overly concerned with his playing and almost afraid to look you in the eye. No doubt there are some easy-going oboe players too, but they are decidedly in the minority. The oboist is a born pessimist, and what makes him so is the ever-present reed problem. No wonder. Here is a treacherous little gadget which he must skillfully carve himself, an incredible two inches of hazard that may make the difference between a solo of heavenly beauty and one that makes everyone cringe! And there are many times when the reed, with the best intentions, simply will not deliver the goods, which leaves the oboist in utter misery. For him the little reed is the center of the universe. When he has a good reed, all creation smiles upon him, and when it is bad, nothing goes right. The late Fritz Busch once said to me, "When you criticize an oboe player for playing a wrong rhythm, he will automatically pull the reed from his instrument and look at it as if it were responsible!"

But the fickleness of the reed is not the oboist's only trouble. In order to blow his instrument properly, he must build up a great deal of air pressure of which he uses only a small amount to produce the tone. The rest of the air presses against his sinus cavities, causing irritation, pain and worse. It is easy to see why a musician who labors under such difficulties should be on edge and hypersensitive. Every conductor should be well aware of this and treat oboists with the greatest gentleness. Even a cross-eyed look from a first oboist should not be taken too seriously. It may be nothing more than an expression of disdain for an inadequate reed!

The other potentially major trouble spot in a symphony orchestra is the French horn section and, more specifically, the first hornist. Here again it is the difficulty and unreliability of the instrument that affects the nerves of the player. Even the finest French horn player is never completely sure of his attack. He may be playing a beautiful melodic line when suddenly a note cracks, to his own dismay and everybody else's! Of course he lives in continuous fear of notes cracking. It is said that Karl Stiegler, for many years the famous first horn of the Vienna Philharmonic, had a standard opening speech for every young man who started to take horn lessons from him. "Before you begin your lessons", he said, "you must know what you are getting into. The French horn is like a woman: when she is not in the mood there is nothing *you* can do!" When a French horn player finishes a beautiful solo in a firm, clear tone, without any accident, it is wise for the conductor to acknowledge it at least with a smile. The hornist himself may feel so triumphant over conquering the natural enemy that the lack of recognition would be a letdown.

With the French horn, there are other problems, too. One of them is pitch, but not individual pitch as much as the coordination of pitch between the four instruments of the section. When the pitch in a horn chord is bad, this is not necessarily a sign of poor sense of pitch or carelessness on anyone's part. Very often, especially in forte chords, it is difficult for the first horn player to hear the exact pitch of the others while he himself plays a loud note. In that case it is a good idea to let the four horns intone their notes in succession, to make them aware of the defect. Frequently an efficient first hornist will do this on his own during intermission.

A further difficulty of the French horn is its notoriously delayed attack, a trait which the player must counteract by playing slightly in advance of the conductor's beat. For the horn players in an orchestra this is a fact of life. Just the same, it is not unusual for the conductor to be treated to a hurt look from the entire horn section when he informs them that their attack in a chord was a shade late. Here, too, it is best to be understanding.

My teacher, Felix Weingartner, used to advise that one should never look directly at a horn player when giving him the entry for an important solo. He himself would in such a case turn his entire body in the other direction, in order not to add to the nervousness of the player. Of course I must state for the record that one very fine first horn player told me that he did not like this method at all. He said he would rather have me look him straight in the eye than notice from my looking away that I was really more concerned over his solo than he was!

It should be remembered that the lips of all brass players tire quite easily, and those of the French horn players considerably more so than the others. For that reason no conductor should try to repeat loud passages of the French horns any more than absolutely necessary. When repetition is unavoidable, it will certainly help his standing with the musicians to ask their indulgence, and thus let them know that he is well aware of their problems. He should also remember that if the horn players seem to "save" during rehearsal (notably during a last rehearsal on the day of the performance), it is not usually a sign of disrespect or indifference, but on the contrary an indication that they wish to preserve their best efforts for the concert.

Considering all the severe technical hazards mentioned, it is not at all surprising that horn players are often temperamental — not aggressive or belligerent like trumpet players, but moody and irritable — and that the leader of the section is frequently referred to as the prima donna of the orchestra. To the novice on the podium this may be somewhat disconcerting. But the best policy seems to be one of flexibility. After all, a prima donna, when properly treated, is likely to give a very thrilling performance!

Once the problems of oboes and French horns have been acknowledged and analyzed, the psychological approach to the rest of the orchestra will be simple by comparison. There are many little idiosyncrasies, but few that ever become dangerous. Flute players suffer from the knowledge that among all the winds they have the greatest difficulty in projecting their tone. A flute solo, therefore, ought to be given special care: the dynamics of the accompanying instruments must be toned down until there is no doubt that the soloist is audible. The piccolo is always loud enough but has a pitch problem that every flute player dreads. Clarinetists are generally eventempered and unpretentious and love to pour their souls into beautiful melodic lines. (I used to know one who, before an important solo, would act like a tenor before an aria!) The only major concern of the clarinetists is the necessity to change quickly from B♭ to A clarinet, or vice versa. If this happens between two movements of a symphony, it is wise for the conductor to make sure that there is enough time for the change. Bassoon players, on the whole, also tend to be pleasant and cooperative. Although they are double reed players, which puts them in the same family with the oboes, they never seem to carry their reed problems on their sleeves in quite the same fashion. Only be considerate when a bassoonist either is required to play a very low note very softly (which sometimes he cannot do) or when he needs to play an extremely high note, no matter at what dynamic level. (The famous high E in Ravel's Piano Concerto in G is a good example, and it makes most first bassoonists tremble in their boots!)

In the brass section, aside from the already mentioned two instruments, there are the trombones and the tuba. The trombones, ordinarily three in number, are not as a rule given extremely difficult technical assignments in symphonic music. When they do encounter great technical hurdles, it is usually due to the fact that an improper instrument is used. For instance, in the opening scene of Verdi's *Otello* there are some treacherous trombone passages. But it is believed that Verdi had in mind the now practically extinct valve trombones, not the slide trombones of our days. There are also some very high and exposed spots for the first trombone in standard literature, not in Strauss or Stravinsky, as one might surmise, but in Beethoven's Fifth and Brahms' Second. Here again the improper instrument is responsible: these passages were written for the now obsolete alto trombone and are played on the tenor trombone at present. It must be said though that most first trombonists, even in lesser orchestras, are quite adept in coping with these problems.

One contingency that deserves the conductor's special attention is the simultaneous entrance of all three trombones in a soft chord, such as in the last movement of Brahms' Fourth. This requires a great deal of relaxation from the players, and a gentle preparation and smooth downbeat from the conductor. Under no circumstances must the conductor make the players nervous by either rushing them into the attack, or by giving a short, angular beat. The result would be lack of precision in the attack and an ugly sound to boot.

My favorite story dealing with this problem concerns the very famous conductor of a major orchestra (this happened some time in the past) who, notwithstanding his other qualities, was never thought of as a virtuoso in technical matters. Once he was rehearsing the above-mentioned passage in Brahms' Fourth. When he arrived at the entrance of the trombones, he gave his inimitable downbeat. In response the three players came in with utter lack of precision, each one having interpreted the conductor's beat in his own way. So the passage was repeated, with the same result; a third time, and again no improvement. By this time the maestro started to mutter curses under his breath. The passage was repeated again, and again, and again, still with no improvement, and with the maestro's curses getting louder after each abortive entrance. By now the mood was on the verge of an explosion. Suddenly the first trombonist had an inspiration. "Watch my foot, boys," he whispered to his two colleagues. That did it. From then on all trombone chords were precise, and the conductor smiled again.

The main psychological problem with tuba players is that they rarely play solos and consequently feel neglected. Since the tuba player works just as hard as any other instrumentalist to keep up his technique, it takes great strength of character on his part not to become a stolid mediocrity. And yet, what a difference the presence of a first rate musician in that assignment can make to the entire orchestra! The conductor can in this case, as in many others, help matters very greatly by giving a little attention in this direction and not treating the player as a necessary evil.*

The problems of the harp are many. Even barely competent harpists are hard

---

* If I did not discuss the problems of such instruments as English horn, E♭ clarinet, bass trumpet, etc., it was not lack of regard for these instruments, but merely the conviction that their difficulties can easily be related to those of their close relatives within the orchestra.

to find since so few people study this beautiful but impractical instrument. Impractical because it is expensive to buy and hard to move from one place to another. And yet, unlike the piano for instance, its possibilities as a solo instrument are very limited. Harpists know that they are hard to replace, and conductors know it too. Therefore, a great deal of patience is indicated. If a clarinetist were to say to the conductor, "Give me time to find the proper key to produce this note," he would not last very long. Nor would a violinist saying, "Give me time to find the right position to play the high E♭." Yet, a harpist in any but the most major orchestras can say without a tinge of selfconsciousness, "Give me time to adjust my pedals!" Also, dynamics on the harp are a sensitive issue. Few and far between are the harp players that play on more than one dynamic level during any given piece of music. I have seen it happen that a harpist, when asked to play a certain spot somewhat louder, would take this as a proof that the conductor simply did not believe in playing piano, and from then on would play everything forte! Perhaps the generosity of most conductors on such occasions is partially motivated by chivalry since most harpists are ladies!

Looking at the strings as a group, the conductor rarely has reason for undue complaint, considering the fact that there are so many of them and that playing as one of many in the rear of a section is not good for one's ego if one had intended to become a virtuoso. As I mentioned before, the conductor who is a competent string player himself quite naturally enjoys better relations with this group. If he is not a string player, he had best lean heavily on an efficient concertmaster, and also he had better not ask for bowings that the players might find impractical. It has always been interesting to me though that string players, in spite of their possibly frustrated personal ambitions, have a tendency to be quite ambitious as a group. I am sure I am not the only conductor to whom it has happened that after he had rehearsed a difficult passage in the violins patiently and slowly a number of times and at last was satisfied with the way it sounded, someone in the ranks would ask to have it repeated once more "just for security's sake."

Although the problems in the string section do not normally exceed what I have already mentioned (the unnatural sitting position, the need to play continuously with hardly any interruptions, and in some cases the difficulties in seeing the conductor's beat), there is one group to which I would give a little special attention: the cellists. Every cellist is a world unto himself. He plays a beautiful instrument which he loves and which to him does not seem to be sufficiently appreciated, nor does it have enough solo literature to suit him. He suffers constantly from the notion that the tone of his instrument does not project properly, particularly on the lower strings, and therefore he has a built-in tendency to play too loud, too expressively, and with too many changes of bow. In these cases the conductor may have to exert a curbing influence. If a French horn player expects an appreciative smile after a beautiful solo, the same is true of an entire cello section after an expressive and prominent melody. Conversely it may sometimes be difficult to convince the cellists that their whole-note alternation of tonic and dominant is less important and should be less prominent than the simultaneous theme in the first oboe. However, to refer again to the instrument-shapes-character theory, just as a harsh, grating sound from a violoncello is unusual, so is it unusual to find an unpleasant or ill-tempered cellist. All he wants is to be heard!

No chapter on orchestra psychology should be written without giving some attention to a very central character, the timpanist. At one time it was fashionable to call the timpanist the "second conductor" of the orchestra. This nickname probably had its foundation in a report that during a performance of Beethoven's Ninth which Richard Wagner led in Bayreuth, things started to go from bad to worse until Hans Richter at the timpani, at that time not yet a famous conductor, took over with an energetic solo and restored order. I have never had much faith in this story since from all reports Wagner was not the type of conductor who needed help from anyone. But the aura has remained, and some timpanists try to live up to it. In a very different vein, in some of my recurring nightmares I see the timpanist as a sour-looking middle-aged man who plays with a pair of sticks of medium size and medium texture, hitting the drums mezzo forte and giving the impression of seasoned mediocrity. Admittedly this is a nightmare, but one not entirely out of touch with reality. It is depressing to think that such things should happen even occasionally when you realize what the contribution of a musically sensitive timpanist to the playing of an orchestra can be. But one should not immediately condemn the timpanist. It is perhaps the conductor who is really the culprit, at least one who treats the timpanist as an also-ran and only starts paying attention to him when he plays too loud or enters at the wrong time. Such an attitude will quite naturally make a cynic out of the timpanist. If, on the other hand, the conductor shows that the sound of the timpani does matter to him, that he would like small and hard sticks in one place, large and soft ones in another, that he wants one approach to timpani playing in Mozart, another in Beethoven, a third in Tchaikovsky and Liszt, a fourth in Stravinsky, to name only a few, then the timpanist who has talent will soon realize his importance and function as the full-fledged member of the orchestra that he should be.

A good timpanist, and one who is encouraged by the conductor, may develop the antics of a showman. When he prepares for a fortissimo roll he may look like a matador coming in for the kill. Personally, I find this much easier to tolerate than the lackadaisical so-what-let's-give-him-another-roll attitude. The timpani are dramatic instruments and should not be played with indifference.

A timpanist can have complexes, too, and they mostly concern pitch. When the conditions of temperature and humidity change, it becomes difficult to tune the drums accurately, but it can be done. We all have heard the first movement of the Beethoven Violin Concerto practically ruined by poorly-tuned timpani in the first measure. In such a case the conductor should be just as strict as he would be about any other pitch lapses.

Whatever the attitude of the conductor, a timpanist is not likely to be overly modest. I learned this during one of my first professional engagements when I had the illustrious task of playing the celesta in a musical comedy. Since my part did not call for very much playing I spent the rest of the time studying scores and watching the timpanist who sat near me. He knew that I was an aspiring conductor. Once, in passing, I told him that I was interested in a certain technique that he used, explaining that I had studied the timpani myself. "What," he exclaimed, "you could be a timpanist? Why then do you want to be a conductor, you fool?"

Chapter 5:

The Rehearsal.

This is the great day: the first rehearsal of the young and relatively inexperienced conductor with a professional orchestra. He has prepared himself to the very best of his ability. He knows the works to be conducted "backwards," as the saying goes (whatever that means!), and although he is not planning to dispense with the scores during rehearsals, he could do so if necessary. He feels as confident of himself as one can under the circumstances. For let there be no doubt about it: complete confidence is an impossibility for the newcomer. The stakes are too high and the risks are too great to feel assured of an easy victory. Even the best-trained soldier does not know before the battle how the enemy is going to act. And to the fledgling on the podium, on the basis of all that he has heard and read, the orchestra must appear as the enemy. To be sure, the first flutist may be his uncle and the third trombonist his bridge partner. But what about all the others?

He may have done his psychological homework too, as I suggested in the preceding chapter. Perhaps he knows something about the personal and professional background of some of the musicians. This could be very important! But still, and above everything, there is the one big question on his mind: *Are they going to like me?* This he will not know until well into the rehearsal, and the agony of the first hour or so should not be underrated.

The musicians are ready in their chairs, presumably with their instruments tuned, and now the young man is introduced to the orchestra by the manager or some other official. He mounts the podium, greeted by polite but perfunctory applause from the musicians. What is the best opening gambit? At one time it was fashionable to make a flattering or witty speech to the orchestra. Now this is obsolete. If it were attempted, nine out of ten musicians would consider it a waste of precious rehearsal time. "Good morning, ladies and gentlemen. Beethoven, please" will do fine. If our novice is the emotional type he may say, "I am happy to be here with you' or some words to that effect. But *not* "It is a privilege to conduct this wonderful orchestra," for flattery automatically makes musicians suspicious. Even though the compliment may be perfectly genuine, to the seasoned player it will sound hypocritical, and its effect will be negative. But whatever the conductor says he should say in a loud, clear voice, for no orchestra trusts a timid leader. He may have to put on an act to do this, for perhaps he feels quite nervous at this juncture. In that case he should make sure that no one but he himself is aware of his nervousness.

A whole chapter could be written about the impression that the young conductor receives when he first looks at the musicians from his elevated vantage point. Put yourself in his place: in front of you there is a sea of faces, and no matter how many orchestras you may have observed from the audience as a listener, or even from a close range when attending a rehearsal, looking at them from the podium, these faces are very different. Part of the difference is in your own mind. You look at them and say to yourself: whatever goes on in these heads will decide my success or failure. So you anxiously try to find a sign of friendliness, perhaps a smile. There may be none. Possibly there is nothing but cold indifference, an expression that seems to say, "Why are you here? We could have done just as well without you!" It may also seem to the conductor that the musicians are hiding behind their instruments or music stands in order to conceal their emotions, a flowery interpretation of the actual facts at best! Again, there may be smiles here and there. "That jolly-looking, round-faced cellist at the third stand smiles at me. He must be on my side! And that boyish-looking second horn player seems like a nice fellow. He would not play any tricks on me! But what about that grinning second trombonist? Is he laughing *with* me or *at* me?."

What does it all amount to? Really very little. Musicians have their ways, and most of them are a regular routine. Not much that happens shortly after a conductor mounts the podium is of significance one way or the other. Practically the only thing that will make the players change is the appearance at the helm of an internationally famous man that they are all in awe of. Then the somewhat blasé attitude of "show us what you can do" is suddenly changed to a humble "please let us show you what *we* can do!" A novice on the podium should realize that he is not going to overwhelm eighty routined men and women in the flutter of an eyelash. Very likely they are willing to perform well for him if his talent and authority warrant it, but they are not going to meet him more than halfway. Conducting is often a war of nerves, and even the best musician cannot become a successful conductor if his nerves will let him down. I am not suggesting that the conductor on the podium should completely disregard the little waves of psychology that reach him from the men and women in the orchestra. But under no circumstances should he let the real or suspected byplay disconcert him. His is a formidable job, and it needs all his energy. If he does it well, recognition will come, even from the orchestra. If not, then all the little tokens of friendship evidenced in nods and smiles will be meaningless.

But since the feelings of the musicians toward the conductor will indicate at least how much initial cooperation he is going to receive from them, we might as well investigate the genesis and causation of those feelings. Richard Strauss' father, the famous horn player of the Munich Opera, has been quoted as saying that a seasoned musician in an orchestra could judge the qualifications of a new conductor "even before he had raised his baton for the first time." This statement makes very good reading, yet it can easily be disproved by the facts. It is undoubtedly true that most of the players form an opinion about the conductor as soon as he appears on the stand. But what Strauss senior does not mention is that this opinion is of necessity superficial and subject to many mutations as soon as the rehearsal starts. When a musician first looks at the conductor he tries to size up his personality, for obviously in a strong conductor there should be signs of a strong personality. However, the weak link in the chain of this conclusion is the fact that the personality projected by the human being may be at variance with the one projected by the artist in his music-making. Thus, a man may have a good figure and excellent posture, combined with striking features and a most winning smile. But when he conducts, his music may be bland and without contours or personality. Another may be ungainly, unsmiling and an obvious introvert. But as soon as he starts to conduct, things begin to happen: the force of his personality becomes apparent, and the music under his hands has conviction and meaning.

It seems to be the consensus of opinion among leading conductors, and also among orchestra musicians, that only the really capable conductor ultimately has any chance of success, and that all other virtues, such as a bright smile, a handsome profile, well tailored clothes or an easy, affable demeanor, must recede into the background as soon as the essential lack of competence of the man is revealed. No doubt this is true. But let us look at the situation from the perspective of the conductor himself. The man with the easy, affable manners will feel after a few minutes that he has established contact with the orchestra because he is a natural extrovert and he always establishes contact with people. Therefore he may believe himself to be well in control of the situation at a time when the musicians have not yet discovered that his tempi are unsteady, his staccato beat mushy, his singing line nervous, and so forth. The opposite type, the unglamorous one, may fail to smile, express himself awkwardly and make a generally unprepossessing impression. As a result there will be snickers here and there and possibly a general tendency not to take him too seriously. He will be sensitive enough to receive all these little signs, and quite possibly he may decide right then and there that he has not "made a hit" with the orchestra, and that therefore the entire venture is doomed to failure. This is, of course, the worst mistake that he could possibly make, for if the musicians had at first only started to doubt his ability, he will now prove to them by his defeatist attitude that they are right. However, if he does possess the indispensable stamina to ignore a few snickers and manages to proceed with unshakable determination, and if this is not only a pose, but if there is also the artistic capability to back up his determination, then the snickers will soon cease, and he may really be in control of the situation and headed for a very good concert — at a time when his more glamorous colleague has already exhausted his resources in the eyes of the musicians.

This attitude of being undaunted in the face of odds is without any doubt the most important one that the conductor must develop. He may or may not have the artistic capacity of a Toscanini. This is something beyond his control.

But at least he can use the capacity that he does possess to the very fullest and not let timidity or nervousness interfere with his work to a point where he appears to the musicians, and also to the audience, much worse than he really is. This has nothing to do with arrogance; no one should try to "give himself airs." Neither should he undersell himself. Innumerable conductors whose artistic ability was or is several shades lower than that of Toscanini (for instance!) have proved that they can make valuable contributions to our musical life if they are sufficiently determined to do so! It must be remembered that a conductor is first and foremost a leader. The rider who lets the reins slacken too much may know the way very well, but he will never get to his destination.

Back to our rehearsal. Let us say that the piece that our young maestro is rehearsing is Beethoven's Seventh Symphony. He starts, and after the first four measures he stops. "Gentlemen," he says, "please give me more espressivo in the first oboe and the first horn, less volume in the second violins and violas, and more precision in the tutti chords." Wrong! The entire statement, although possibly musically justified, turns out to be a serious psychological mistake. As far as the espressivo is concerned, it is not of worldshaking importance and could easily have been requested either after a substantial portion of the movement, say the entire introduction, had been played, or perhaps before the next playing of the beginning of the symphony, assuming optimistically that this is not a one-performance, one-rehearsal proposition. The volume in the second violins and violas needed no mention at all — it could have been controlled by a simple restraining motion of the left hand. And as to the precision of the chords, the answer is supplied by the outside man on the third stand of the violas, who grinningly says to his desk neighbor, "Let him give us a better upbeat, and we'll give him more precision!"

However, the *real* mistake of the conductor was to stop so soon. The first rehearsal of a new man on the podium should start with an attempt of conductor and players to "feel each other out." For that purpose it is necessary to play a sizeable section of the music without interruption, something which in the case of a well known Classical symphony should be possible without major disasters. The orchestra will appreciate these tactics. It will give the musicians a chance, at least in a basic sense, to find out what the new man wants, and more importantly, if he really knows what he wants. This he can indicate much better by his conducting gestures than by verbal instructions. And who knows, by the time the orchestra has played for five minutes without a stop, the musicians may have warmed up to him! This is not to say that major discrepancies should be left unheeded, *major* ones, mind you! Every orchestra reacts with irritability to unnecessary stops. It is wise for the conductor to remember that if he has enough rehearsal time with the orchestra to play a piece three times, each time allowing for a number of interruptions, he should not try to make all his corrections during the first reading. The first time through is best devoted to establishing the general outlines of his interpretation, and to correcting mistakes of so serious a nature that to tolerate them would make the musicians lose their ambition and also make them lose their respect for the technical standards of the leader.

Often it is not easy for a conductor, particularly an inexperienced one, to decide whether he should stop to correct a mistake or continue and mention it when a natural interruption offers itself at the end of a section. It is just as bad to stop for a trifling slip of one musician which he himself noticed as soon as he had made it, to make a pedantic correction and thus perhaps humiliate and antagonize the musician in question, as it is to let a sloppy attack of several instruments, a severe lapse of pitch in an entire group, or an obviously wrong harmony go by as if nothing had happened. Perhaps it will be helpful at this point to classify mistakes or discrepancies occurring during orchestra rehearsals roughly into four groups, according to their origin and severity:

1. Careless misreading of notes, octave signs, trills etc. by single individuals. No interruption is necessary. The musician in question will either indicate by a nod of the head that he has noticed his mistake, or else his attention can be called to it by a single word from the conductor while the playing continues. For instance, if a bassoonist erroneously reads bass clef instead of tenor clef, the conductor, without stopping, should turn in his direction and say "tenor clef." This should take care of the situation.

2. The omission of dynamic signs, such as crescendo, diminuendo, subito piano, accents etc. by either individuals or groups, or the execution of these signs in a manner not in accord with the interpretative ideas of the conductor, too much or too little. In this case again the conductor should not stop but simply make a mental note. When a natural break, such as the end of a section or movement, has been reached he should leaf through the preceding section in the score and mention all these discrepancies. If at the next reading one or several of them occur again, then it will be necessary to stop and make the correction immediately. Much of this will depend on the routine and professional caliber of the orchestra.

3. Mistakes made by individuals, and sometimes also by groups, that they are obviously not aware of: an entrance on the second quarter when it should be on the third, a wrong note that is not immediately noticeable, a forte where there should be a piano, a non legato where there should be staccato, and similar errors. In these cases more often than not the fault lies with incorrect or poorly legible parts, and it is much wiser to stop and clear the matter up once and for all than to glare at the offending musician each time the passage is played, and have him reply with a hurt look since he is utterly unaware that there is anything wrong.

4. Shortcomings of execution that are not based on any particular misreadings of notes or rhythms, or on the failure to observe signs, but mostly on lack of technical capability or polish; sometimes also on failure to interpret the musical substance correctly, or at least to interpret it in accordance with the conductor's ideas. These are the principal contingencies to which rehearsal time will be devoted. Frequently it may be necessary to change a bowing in the strings,

or a breath mark in the winds. If it is a difficult technical passage, it might require slow group-by-group practice (something which string players particularly mind a great deal less than the novice conductor is inclined to expect!). It may also be necessary to pencil in corrections of dynamic marks in order to rectify an improper balance. Here again the novice at the helm should not be shy: it is much less essential that every mezzo forte in the second trumpet actually be played as a mezzo forte than that the composer's ideas be made to emerge in the clearest and most persuasive fashion! Any of these aforementioned occurrences will necessitate an immediate stopping and a careful explanation of what must be corrected. It is only to be hoped that from one rehearsal to the next the number of stops will decrease, so that the final rehearsal may sound, to all intents and purposes, like a performance.

It can easily be seen from the preceding that the greatest number of stops and repeats will occur in the middle of the rehearsing period. In the beginning, a certain amount of continuous playing should establish the musical values to be striven for, and more so if conductor and orchestra do not know each other or if the piece rehearsed is either completely new or has not been played by the orchestra for some time. After that comes the time for what musicians love to refer to as "woodshedding": the repeating of difficult passages until they feel completely secure and the balancing, polishing and refining of sounds. Once this has been done to a reasonable degree, it is wise to think of the element of continuity, especially in the case of a full-length symphony. When a musician has some technical problems in a work, it is not sufficient to solve them one by one. He must also get the "feel" of playing them in correct sequence with no relaxing breaks in between. This is the main purpose of the last rehearsal: it must give the correct "feel" of playing the works, so that nothing in the performance will surprise the musicians except perhaps the audience!*

Another important rule that should be observed during the last rehearsal, provided that there is time to do so, is to play the selections in the correct order in which they are to be played in the concert. There may be some very special reasons for this. For instance, in a concert that I conducted recently, the same musician was called upon to play the tenor saxophone in one piece and the E♭ clarinet in another. Naturally he would have been very unhappy had the last rehearsal not been played in the correct order, for the change from tenor saxophone to E♭ clarinet feels physically very different from the reverse procedure.

---

* Since only a comparatively small number of American symphony orchestras are fully staffed with professional players, it is natural to ask how the professional musician differs in his behavior during rehearsals and performance from the amateur or semiprofessional musician. In my view it is not so much that the professional plays better (which he does in most cases, although by no means always) or even that he is technically more reliable, which is generally true since he can devote more time to practice. The most important difference to me seems to be the element of concentration during rehearsals: to the professional, you say during the first rehearsal, "I wait slightly before this downbeat," and he will wait with you every time. The amateur may have to be reminded two or three more times before he remembers.

But even if there are no special reasons of this kind, with the exception of a few virtuoso orchestras, every orchestra will benefit from playing the entire program in order with no interruptions, except perhaps the repeating of a few spots at the end of the playing of each individual piece. But what in my opinion is of paramount importance is that the last rehearsal must open with the first piece on the program. Often such a piece may present serious pitch problems (for instance, Beethoven's *Consecration of the House* overture) which might grow to disastrous proportions if the playing of the piece as a first number — "cold", as it were — had not been faced at least once.

There are a few other rules that might profitably be followed. Corrections should always be made in as few words as possible, and they should be specific, addressed only to the instrument or group of instruments that they are meant for, and in terms that each musician can easily understand. No sentence addressed to an orchestra should ever start with the word "somehow," such as "somehow this movement isn't light enough" or "somehow this does not have the expression that I want." Instead, such impressionistic statements should be translated into technical language: "for this group of instruments a change from mezzo forte to piano, for that other the quarter-notes played more staccato," etc. Verbal picture painting, such as "give me the glow of a sunset in August" is generally suspect and would be disastrous if used by a beginner. A conductor who knows his musicians very well may occasionally and on the spur of the moment use a simple, clear image that will catch the musician's fancy and thus produce the desired result — "a cascading waterfall," "mosquitoes buzzing" — but the novice who cannot as yet anticipate reactions had better stay away from it and remain faithful to the accredited terms of dynamics and phrasing that are taught in our conservatories.

It is a well known fact that orchestras all over the world dislike conductors who talk too much. Of course it is not always easy to decide just how much is "too much." But in case of doubt, less is better than more. If a conductor spontaneously thinks of a subject-related witty remark in the middle of a rehearsal, there is no reason why he should suppress it. However, the keyword is "spontaneously." Orchestras are notably suspicious of conductors who spend half their time thinking up witticisms, which then are usually not very witty. But even when it comes to serious thoughts and ideas, if they are not indispensable to the work at hand, they had better be kept out. That marvelous anecdote about what conductor X said during a rehearsal in Chicago fifty years ago will sound delightful over a cup of coffee during the rehearsal break where it may even serve the psychological purpose of a rapprochement between conductor and orchestra. But on paid rehearsal time it is a luxury, and an expensive one.

Let us return once more to the psychological ordeal that faces the inexperienced conductor when he conducts a professional or even a semi-professional orchestra. He may have had excellent technical training, may have received advice from the best sources, may have studied all the rules of behavior from books such as this, and yet it is still likely to be a shattering experience. The young conductor who says after his first, or for that matter, after any of the first dozen orchestra rehearsals that he conducts, "It went fine: they gave me everything that I wanted" is either a fool or a liar. There may be moments of easy triumph, when a vigorous, resilient downbeat elicits a crisp, clear chord from the orchestra, or when a calmingly raised left hand produces a beautiful, tender pianissimo. But this will not cause the sensitive musician on the podium to overlook the fact that there was a great deal that he could not control and that did not function in the fashion that he had anticipated. Bruno Walter, in his autobiographical *Theme and Variations,* tells in a remarkable bit of soul-searching how after years of accumulating excellent conducting experience, he reached a point where he felt completely unsure of his own technique and where every pizzicato and every fortissimo chord caused him serious concern. He describes how it took years of the most rigorous disciplining process to overcome these weaknesses. If this can happen to one of the truly outstanding men in the profession, it is obvious that it must happen to the man of average talent to a far greater degree, although not every conductor will admit the existence of such difficulties as freely as Bruno Walter. These are some of the factors that make conducting so difficult, and there is no shortcut by which the obstacles can be overcome. There is only trying, soul-searching, correcting and trying again until the enemy is finally conquered.

One of the young conductor's greatest problems, and therefore also greatest apprehensions, is the ability to listen analytically, i.e. to be able to detect wrong notes in a maze of sound. The anecdotes that deal with this important topic are too well known to be mentioned here. But, stories or no stories, the importance of the matter remains paramount, not so much for practical purposes as for reasons of prestige, for in actuality most wrong notes are taken care of without the conductor's intervention. After all, the musician also has ears, and when his note does not fit into the chord, he will probably either ask a question or check his part with the orchestra score. So by the time the conductor wishes to make the correction, the matter may already have been attended to. However, if the musician who played the wrong note very pointedly asks the question in the presence of the entire orchestra, and from the conductor's reply it becomes apparent that nothing amiss had occurred to him, then his prestige will obviously suffer. The most dangerous contingency as far as the conductor is concerned would be a wrong note "planted" on purpose, to make fun of his inability to detect it. However, in order not to cause the tyro too many sleepless nights, I shall say that according to my experience these tricks are not played very often in our days. Musicians of today are generally businesslike, and they are first and foremost interested in getting the job done, not in playing tricks.

But the question remains: why does it happen that a conductor who, if he were sitting in the auditorium with his score listening to an orchestra, would say at a certain point, "The note in the second clarinet should be C, not C#, and that the same conductor remains unaware of this discrepancy when he stands on the podium? Erich Leinsdorf explains that "the inexperienced conductor, when on the podium, is completely overwhelmed by the situation. His heart starts beating too fast, and thus he misses the most obvious mistakes in the playing." Assuming, as I do, that this is an amazingly accurate description of what actually happens, the only answer is to exercise the utmost self-control and to keep one's heart from beating too fast, which is admittedly easier said than done.

However, I believe that there is another side to this problem. Furtwängler once stated that "generally considered, there is no such thing among conductors as a good or bad ear. There is only a greater or lesser mastery of the material, that is, the score and its every detail. One can only hear individual mistakes in the complicated mass of sound when one knows completely just what the composer wanted."* I find this very convincing, although it must be borne in mind that there could be quite a gap between "knowing completely just what the composer wanted" and being able to pinpoint the perhaps elusive mistake that separates the actual sound from the one that is projected by the score. Without question, a conductor in his formative years must avail himself of every opportunity to cope with these problems. Leinsdorf suggests that the young adept ought to coach a small ensemble, such as a string quartet, to learn how to detect mistakes on one hand, and on the other to find ways of correcting them in the quickest and most efficient fashion.

Another subject that requires clarification is the attitude of the musicians themselves. What do they expect from a new conductor? Godfrey Layefsky, for many years first violist of the Pittsburgh Symphony, answered this question with one word: "communication." Striking as this answer may be, it should not be overlooked that there are two separate aspects to communication: the substance to be communicated and a method by which to communicate it. The substance is largely a matter of native talent and musicianship. The conductor must be involved with the music that he conducts, otherwise his work will be nothing but undistinguished time beating. But he must also possess a clear and precise method to get his substance or message across, and that is what we usually call technique. A musician in the orchestra wants to sense the conductor's deep concern with the music that he conducts, but he must also see a beating pattern that allows for easy and secure technical orientation. Without this latter type of accomplishment, the conductor is likely to become a "dancing dervish." No doubt he feels the music deeply, but since he lacks an acceptable method of controlling the orchestra through his beat, the results are likely to be deplorable.

Sometimes a conductor may feel that the concern over a clean technique may cut down the eloquence of his emotional message, and conversely that the urge to express his emotions to the fullest could result in a muddy technique. This may be so, but it need not be so. It is true that both extremes are found. And while the technically perfect but emotionally shallow conductor may fascinate us at first, but after a while generates no more interest than a violinist who can play a Paganini caprice with hair-raising virtuosity but whose Mozart

---

* As quoted by Albert Stoessel in *The Technique of the Baton* (Carl Fischer, 1928).

and Beethoven are dull, the other extreme does and always did have some representatives among the first rank of conductors. The conductor whose spiritual power is so great that he has the ability to show a thrice familiar score, without trying to be "original," in a compelling new light, may sometimes tend to disregard the technical side of his profession and still obtain most remarkable results. Furtwängler was probably the best example. But even Furtwängler was said to have done by far his best work with orchestras that knew him intimately well. Others had a certain amount of trouble understanding his beat. Surely for the beginner this is far too heady a diet, and even an inclination in that direction could destroy his career before it has properly started. Anyone who feels even for one moment that the adherence to a clear beat could be a hindrance to expressing himself with full emotional freedom should remember that Toscanini, Weingartner, Monteux, and any number of other top-ranking men in the same category, were never ashamed of their technique.

At this point another contingency deserves to be mentioned. The conductor who in his formative years was taught a clear beat will gradually learn to rely on it as an automatic feature of his physical behavior, and he will be able to concentrate more and more on problems of musical communication without the fear of losing precision in the playing of the orchestra. But it must be said that the virtue of a clear beat can be grossly exaggerated, and that the over-emphasis on clear beating may annoy the musicians as being scholastic and sterile. A musician likes to be led with assurance, but he does not like to have the conductor "on his neck" all the time, particularly not in the playing of an expressive romantic solo. Weingartner, in a second-hand description of Wagner's conducting, makes the most illuminating observation that when Wagner conducted "the players had no sense of being led. Each believed himself to be following freely his own feeling. Each thought himself free, while in reality he only followed the leader, whose artistic force lived and worked in him."

Without trying to downgrade for one moment the necessity of beating clearly, my own experience has taught me that often the best results are obtained not so much by the beating pattern as by an unbendable inner conviction as to how the music should sound. This may be telepathy, but it works! Particularly in rubato passages where the musical pattern is so fluid that even the clearest beat cannot control every detail of the execution, the conductor who has the courage to relax his beat to some extent, while at the same time allowing the passage to sing in his inner ear with the utmost conviction, will often triumph over fearful technical difficulties. One need only remember Monteux, who frequently was able to produce the utmost in technical and musical clarity by means of an almost careless beat.

A great deal of the conductor's craft is learned by observing other conductors. I remember well how we conducting students in Vienna would sneak into the balcony through forbidden doors in order to watch Toscanini, Furtwängler, Walter or Klemperer in rehearsal. Naturally, when you observe great masters at the time in your life when you are most impressionable, you are almost automatically driven to imitation. Needless to say you will imitate the conductor whom you admire most. Of course there is nothing wrong with absorbing the procedures of a master and later applying them to one's own use. But imitation unfortunately often extends to other matters: in our youthful enthusiasm we may try to imitate how the great man held his ears when the pitch in the winds was wrong, or how he slammed the score on the stand when the precision was not up to his standards. That such mannerisms are not the best method to win friends and influence people in the orchestra when you are young and inexperienced need hardly be stated. But this is not the only reason why they should be avoided: every imitation sooner or later leads to dullness and sterility. For better or for worse, a conductor has his own personality, and that is the only one he can work with. He can discipline it and try to develop its best potentialities, but it would be foolhardy to try to reshape it in somebody else's image.

"Image!" A magic word in our days. "What image do I wish to project?" the young conductor may ask himself when he steps in front of an orchestra for the first time. The various books give you all kinds of advice: you should be strict but not dictatorial, you should be friendly but not chummy, you should earn respect from the orchestra rather than demand it, and so forth. So every young conductor tries to project a glorified image of himself, possibly an image that may have little or no connection with the basic realities of his own character. He strives to impress the musicians with one or the other striking quality that he has observed in one of his conductorial idols until he finds out (if he is intelligent enough!) that he is what he is and that every attempt to disguise this fact is quickly recognized by the orchestra as a fake. Thus, I feel that the projecting of an "image" is one clumsy detour that the novice could do without. There is not one way of working with an orchestra, not even three or four. There are dozens or hundreds of ways, and the only one that works for you is the one that fits *your* personality. What Erich Leinsdorf does in rehearsal may work wonders for Erich Leinsdorf. But if Hamilton Farnsworth Jones should foolishly try to use the same technique, he would quickly run aground. The only legitimate image that I can project is my own, and that will project itself naturally if I will only let it! It all boils down to the same basic truth: in our day more than ever, the conductor is not expected to be a sorcerer or snake-charmer but a secure craftsman and a sincere artist. If he will only concentrate on these qualities to the best of his ability, then the image will undoubtedly take care of itself.

INTERLUDE 3:
The Visual Aspect.

Let it be said again that this is not a book on conducting technique. This technique as such, which is only of tangential interest to our investigation, could be explained as the ability to translate the printed symbols in the orchestra score into visual symbols expressed through the conductor's movements, which in turn can be translated into the actual sounds played by the orchestra. Of all this, while avoiding the hard-core problems of time beating and its concomitants, we cannot ignore the visual effect of the conductor's physical demeanor since the impact of the physical is, of necessity, psychological. The conductor himself is seen, and only the music that he controls is heard. So it is quite natural that his appearance and everything he does physically from the moment of his first entrance are bound to influence orchestra and audience. Such matters cannot be treated lightly.

Let us begin with the audience. Is it not rather shallow to weigh the visual impact that the conductor exerts on the people in the hall who have come to hear the music? Will this not detract from his essential purpose, which is being the spokesman and interpreter of the composer? And will it not encourage the idea of viewing him as a glamorous, show-conscious movie actor-type of performer who brings the crowd under his spell by the magnetic beauty of his dance-like movements, so that it is perhaps no longer the music that enthralls the listeners, but its compelling visualization in the conductor's gestures?

I think not. Executing a gesture in a visually pleasing fashion and trying to attract attention to this gesture (and away from the music!) are two entirely different things. Since the conductor moves in full view of the listeners (or spectators, as it were) it is well for him not to antagonize them visually. There is no conceivable advantage in appearing gauche and ungainly. It must be realized though that unpleasant appearance and demeanor are not the same as a musically prompted freedom of movement that may lead to the abandonment of traditional technical patterns. A Furtwängler, through his inspiration as a musician, was often driven toward gestures that cannot be found in any textbook of conducting. In spite of that, his movements, although highly unconventional, were harmonious and far from awkward.

Of course, not every conductor has the same potential for visual grace and beauty, nor is there any need for such standardization. Yet I do not recall a single master of the first rank who would distract or repel the audience by his clumsy gestures. My own teacher, Felix Weingartner, who was undoubtedly one of the most elegant and physically perfect conductors of all times, used to become very irritated when it was even mildly insinuated that this might be showmanship on his part. "Should I feel self-conscious," he would say, "because I happen to be well-built?" Or "should I purposely employ ugly gestures, so that I can clear myself of the suspicion of being a showman-conductor?" Perhaps Weingartner did sometimes go a little further in the direction of perfect outward appearance than absolutely necessary. If so, it was a small failing as measured against his enormous accomplishments as a musician.

Obviously it is ludicrous to suggest that a distinguished musician's absorption in his music should cause him to neglect his appearance and gestures to the point of repulsiveness. Presenting an acceptable exterior does not indicate shallowness or vanity, merely respect for the presence of an audience — the same respect that one would expect from a public speaker, a banker, or any other professional who has extended dealings with the public. Not long ago I attended a concert where the conductor, not endowed by nature with too many physical virtues, entered the stage in an ill-fitting dress suit, at a slouchy gait, and with a generally despondent demeanor. It would have taken the musical magic of a Toscanini to counteract effectively the unfavorable impression of his entrance. However, let it be stated for the record that this man did not subsequently "disappoint" the audience: the projection of his entire physical performance on the podium was just as negative as that of his entrance, and it would have been surprising should anyone in the hall have concluded that the maestro was too great a musician to pay attention to external matters.

Not every conductor is endowed with the looks of a Greek god. But that is no reason why even the least prepossessing one should neglect his appearance or be despondent over it. The conductor's podium in a concert hall has a tendency to exaggerate a man's looks: he can look better than his best if he really tries, and worse than his worst if he does not! If he happens to be short, then he should, with the greatest amount of conviction, pull himself up to the full height of his five feet two inches and exude strength and radiance, and most of all, convey to everyone his own joy in making music. Toscanini, Walter, Koussevitzky and Monteux were all short men, and they all looked most dignified, not to say majestic, when they conducted. In our days the music must come first, and we can no longer don black gloves for the conducting of the Funeral March from the "Eroica," as Bülow reportedly did, but we are still expected to present the best exterior of which we are capable. Learning to stand erect and to refrain from making jerky or sloppy gestures is as important as learning to beat a clear four-four time, and once it has been learned it becomes instinctive and need not be given further consideration.

But if the external behavior and the mannerisms of a conductor are important in relation to the audience, they are infinitely more important in relation to the orchestra. The listener in the fifteenth row may find it enjoyable to watch the conductor, but if not he may close his eyes. The musician in the orchestra is not so lucky. He is obliged to keep his eyes on the conductor at all times, and therefore the difference in the latter's physical manifestations to him may be the difference between a most pleasant experience and a nightmare. For it must be said that even to the esthetically less than hypersensitive person it is no joy to focus his vision on a maestro who continuously waves his arms like the propellers of a windmill, who accompanies every retard with an audible groan or who, in the quest for expression, distorts his face as if fiery tongs were being applied to his epidermis. Once, during the intermission of an opera rehearsal, I went into a neighboring tavern and found there a violinist of the orchestra who had just ordered a double Scotch.

"What," I said with surprise, "you can drink this while you work?"

"That is the only way I don't get sick looking at Maestro X's clumsy gestures," was the somewhat ill-humored reply.

However, one should try to understand the musicians' motivations. It is not that they want to see an Apollo of the Belvedere on the podium, although in the case of some of the ladies in the orchestra this latter contingency should not be completely discounted. Their reason is that the physical control and expressiveness of the leader tells the musicians in the most eloquent way how he would like to have the music performed. It is only natural that if the musicians must look at a conductor who expresses himself physically in a clumsy and awkward fashion, they may easily be driven toward playing the music in a fashion that sounds clumsy and awkward. In the light of this the old joke about "if you are not going to be nicer to us we shall play the way you conduct" takes on an entirely new meaning! We often resent ungainly stage mannerisms in a pianist or violinist. There they may be distracting to the audience, but at least they are not likely to interfere with the quality of the music. With a conductor the situation is far more serious since he operates only partially through manual skill and mainly through skillful psychology. Therefore, no matter how great a musician he may be, his gawkiness will somehow be reflected in the finished product, the sounds that are produced by the orchestra.

The problem is not entirely an esthetic one though. When a conductor drives himself to a frenzy over the music that he conducts, this may prove eloquently that he is not impervious to the music's stirring message, but it also hinders him in his most important duty: the control of the orchestra.* The musicians are basically matter-of-fact people: although they do like to find expressions of conviction and individuality in their leader's behavior, what they need more than anything else is a sense of orientation and clarity. No one in an orchestra can play with an all-consuming passion if he is not sure when the beat of four ought to occur. When there is more passion than control, the man at the helm may never be aware that his own dithyrambic vision of the music is only very lamely equated by the muddy and undisciplined playing of the orchestra. He may dream himself into an overwhelming orgy of crashing fortissimos and not notice that the oboes came in two bars too soon! And if things get too much out of control, even the audience may be disillusioned. The orchestra will certainly not respect a leader, no matter how inspired, who lets the technical side of the music go to pot.

This leads us toward one of the most discussed problems of our profession: how much — or how little — should the conductor move on the podium? There is really no hard and fast rule, but perhaps some clarity can be gained by asking what must be accomplished, and how it can be accomplished in the most efficient and direct fashion.

During his adolescent years, every budding conductor finds himself practicing his gestures in front of a mirror, and at that age he is very likely to give it all he has, at least physically. He may wallow in the feeling of strength that it gives him to throw both fists in the air for a brass cue, he may stretch out his arms to the utmost to make a string melody sing ecstatically, or he may skip on his

---

* I am fond of the story told about a rather well known conductor who during a concert that he conducted allegedly drove himself to such physical exertion that he fell off the podium and was saved from a bad accident only by the presence of mind of the concertmaster who caught him in his arms.

61

heels to produce the effect of a resilient staccato in the woodwinds. This is what the dream of conducting means to him: abandon yourself completely to the physical and spiritual passion of the music, and through your unbounded frenzy arouse those pedestrian musicians from their lethargy to a point where they *must* follow you in your ride to the clouds! How tremendously exhilarating it is when the final fortissimo chord thus arrives in a blaze of glory! And how exhausting!*

It does not take most fledgling maestri very long to change their adolescent views on this subject and to realize that economy of gesture is, if nothing else, a necessity for survival. Furthermore, routined musicians are easily amused by the exaggerated physical antics of a novice conductor. Their first undisguised chuckles during rehearsal will undoubtedly serve to return the young man to reality and to remind him that he is to lead an orchestra and not to perform a sacrificial dance. As he matures, he will gradually learn the deep satisfaction that can be derived from a restrained physical behavior in front of the orchestra. This has nothing whatever to do with becoming more moderate in one's musical demands — on the contrary! If in one rehearsal I feel that I must tense every muscle in my body to the utmost in order to obtain the full intensity of a certain orchestral climax, and in the next rehearsal, after some soul-searching on my part, I can get the same intense climax with my physical effort cut in half, then I am bound to be pleased. The conductor who has learned how to produce a powerful fortissimo without clenched fists, and without every muscle in his arms tightened to the breaking point has already learned a great deal about the psychological mechanics of conducting. As Franz Liszt expressed it: "The real task of the conductor is to make himself *ostensibly* quasi useless." Which means that the utmost effect should be accomplished with a minimum of physical energy, so that it appears as if the conductor were releasing rather than producing the prodigious sounds emanating from the orchestra. This is perhaps not in line with the favorite ideas of a youthful romantic on the podium, but it is eminently practical, and in the long run eminently satisfying.

After a number of years of conducting, and thereby gaining insight into the psychological processes of the activity, the mature baton wielder's attitude is likely to be the exact opposite of that of the fist-throwing youngster in front of his mirror. He has learned, like Liszt, that physical abandon achieves nothing, and he knows how important it is to be in control all the time. But aside from that he would like to feel that after a number of hours of rehearsal with the orchestra the musicians will be sufficiently familiar with his ideas to make the continuous emphasizing by gesture unnecessary. The expressive details should then take care of themselves. Max Rudolf worded this most convincingly when

---

* Once in Weingartner's conducting class a new entrant tried to impress the master with this very type of wild histrionics. Weingartner interrupted him, smiled, and said, "Young man, if you should ever conduct *Götterdämmerung* in this fashion, you will need three weeks of vacation afterwards!" After this episode all the students in the class used restrained and economical gestures.

he said, "The conductor should not work for anything which the orchestra is willing to provide by its own initiative."

Shortly before his death, Dimitri Mitropoulos conducted a concert in New Orleans which I attended, and in which the featured symphony was Kabalevsky's Fourth. In one of its movements a march rhythm builds up in a frenzied crescendo to an extremely roaring climax while the tempo remains constant. Mitropoulos set an exact speed and engineered a most dramatic buildup. When the fortissimo was reached, he suddenly stopped conducting and did not resume his motions for at least thirty measures, while the orchestra continued its ear-shattering dithyramb. Perhaps this was showmanship, but the effect was absolutely spellbinding, and it is unlikely that any physical exertion on the conductor's part could have brought the movement to such an overwhelming climax.

So much for the basic principle of physical passion versus economy of movement. Beyond that it stands to reason that the work of a competent and artistic conductor involves far more in a physical respect than the mere ability to remain in control, move economically and appear reasonably graceful at all times. If the conductor's gestures are to inspire the musicians with the proper expression, then the expression should in some way be found in the gestures themselves. It is often said critically that the conductor must not be a "dancer." Dancing is an activity that is an end in itself, not designed to inspire and control another activity. Conducting, on the other hand, is merely a means to an end. However, every really fine conductor is a dancer in the sense that his body must be a subtly tuned instrument, sensitive to the finest vibrations of the music and capable of translating them into a palpable visualization, one that the musician can readily understand. Only we expect this visualization to be so restrained in nature that to the average person the suggestion of "dancing" will not occur.

The necessary subtlety of expression begins with the conductor's stance. When he strikes us as awkward, the first (even though subconscious) impression is probably that of a faulty stance. Naturally, different conductors will choose different stances, and it must not be implied that one is always wrong and the other always right. A great deal will depend on the style and character of the music, and a stance that will suit the polka from *The Bartered Bride* perfectly would look shockingly out of place in the conducting of Mozart's G Minor Symphony.

For the sake of orientation I should like to classify opera and symphony conductors into four categories, according to their preferred stances:

1. Legs and heels together, both heels in one line parallel with the footlights, feet pointing outward at approximately a 45° angle from each other. This is roughly comparable to the military "position of attention." One might call it the "classic" stance: it combines controlled strength with grace and elegance, making it a perfect stance for the conducting of symphonies of the Viennese classical school. Conductors who favor it are usually the ones whose forte lies in the German standard repertoire from Haydn to Brahms. Weingartner immediately

comes to mind as one of its most perfect practitioners. It is probable that this stance is practiced by far the greatest number of serious orchestral conductors, for the reason that although it may be more suited to certain types of music than to others, it will never look completely out of place.

2. Legs about a foot apart, heels again in one line parallel with the footlights. This stance, which is esthetically extremely unsuitable for short, sinewy men may look very well when taken by someone tall and broadshouldered. It will also be helpful in balancing the weight of a more corpulent conductor. One might call it the "romantic" stance: exuding reposeful strength and a certain majestic quality, it is best suited to the conducting of Bruckner, Wagner (Meistersinger-Prelude!), Sibelius, most of Shostakovich, and also some major choral works, such as the *Missa Solemnis* or the Brahms Requiem. It would look strange in Mozart's "Jupiter" Symphony, but even stranger in Stravinsky's *Petrouchka*, or Bartok's *Concerto for Orchestra*. This stance is seen in the photographs of Hans Richter, and Fritz Busch favored it very strongly. Often it is thought of as "Germanic," but this may be a fallacy. Pierre Monteux, for instance, used it quite frequently.

3. Legs fairly close together, but one foot farther forward than the other, with the weight of the body resting on the front foot (rarely and not very advantageously it may also rest on the back foot). This might be called the "dynamic" stance. It creates the illusion of the body being in forward motion, and it is most often assumed by tall, slim conductors whose preponderant concern is excitement. It is the exact opposite of the romantic stance, and it lends itself to most contemporary works, but also to the later Beethoven, Brahms, Tchaikovsky and Strauss. Furtwängler used it often, so did Knappertsbusch. In our day Karajan and Bernstein can be observed using it.

4. The "flexible" stance, which is really a combination of the three preceding ones, and which changes very quickly in character according to the character of the music. These changes are often accentuated by a quick shifting of the body weight. Best suited for conductors of medium build and better than average physical agility, it is the least image-creating of the four, and it adjusts very easily to any type of music.

It is not suggested that any conductor should or does assume any of the first three stances all the time. This would be quite unnatural. Therefore it would seem at first glance that the flexible stance may be deemed superior to all others since it does not predetermine the physical expression. This is not necessarily true. Many conductors are of such a build that any attempt to look physically flexible would appear artificial and perhaps ludicrous. We are dealing here with factors of body structure that cannot be ignored. We can observe the same phenomenon when one man walks into a clothing store, tries on the first suit of his size and finds that it fits him perfectly. Another will either need many alterations, or he will only be able to wear a suit tailored to his measurements. Similarly, the principle of types also holds true in matters of musical interpretation. One conductor is marvelous in Beethoven or Brahms, but his Debussy will be stale and square. Another will generate a great deal of excitement in Ravel or Stravinsky, but his Mozart strikes you as erratic or tasteless. And then — rarely — there is the musician of universal talent who can adjust his personality to all kinds of styles and yet lend to each of them the full impact of his own individual approach.

If the stance is of great importance in projecting the character of the music, the expressive quality of the beat itself is even more essential. Nothing can be as boring and disillusioning to a fine orchestra as a square, unrefined beat that never varies in size, intensity or expression. The orchestra conductor of genuine talent will either know instinctively or be able to learn how to "orchestrate" his beat: he will adjust it not only to the expression of any particular phrase, but also to the instrument or group of instruments that plays it. This is a rather sophisticated process, and many conductors of otherwise sizeable accomplishments remain essentially incapable of it. Perhaps the primary consideration in achieving this technique is to give every instrumentalist a type of movement that suggests in some way his own physical approach to his instrument. A typical example is the long, sweeping motion that many conductors use in a broadly sung string passage that requires the forceful use of the entire bow, or the short flick of the wrist that is used to conduct a pizzicato chord. Not all suggestions can be made so directly, but at least the player's physical sensation can in many cases be duplicated. Thus, a fanfare-like entrance in the trumpets will be given by a sharp, short stroke of the forearm with taut muscles. A pianissimo chord in the trombones, on the other hand, will be signaled through a completely relaxed, floating motion of the entire arm, a cantabile solo in the first oboe with a rounded pull of the wrist of very limited diameter, and so forth. This is the type of technical approach for which the musicians will be grateful. They are highly individualistic in their music making, and they want the conductor to allow clearly for this circumstance. One reason why choral conductors so often fare badly in conducting orchestras is that they generally do not allow for the physical differences in the approach to the various instruments and conduct an orchestra as if it were a group of singers, all producing the same type of sound.

It hardly needs mention that the beat should also amply account for the difference in style between works of different periods. Conducting 44 musicians in a Mozart symphony where the dynamic range is limited by the style, the radius of movement will quite naturally be much smaller than in conducting 95 musicians in a symphony by Mahler. But there is also a physical difference suggested by the phrase itself: the graceful gentleness of the Andante cantabile from Beethoven's First Symphony will suggest to the sensitive maestro a spatially much more restrained beat than the heartrending tearfulness of the finale of Tchaikovsky's *Pathétique*! The beginning of the Scherzo from Mendelssohn's *A Midsummer Night's Dream* and the beginning of Strauss' *Don Juan* both have a jumping quality, but they compare with each other as the jump of a kitten compares with that of a racehorse. All this must be expressed in the infinite

65

variety of the conductor's beating patterns, and when it is all there, then we may refer to him as a skillful, sensitive technician.

During my student days one of the leading newspapers in Vienna entertained its readers by polling a few of the leading conductors of the day on their opinions regarding the amount of physical movement that a conductor should use on the podium. Unfortunately the intervening years have blotted out in my memory most of this undoubtedly fascinating controversy, but I do remember very vividly Wilhelm Furtwängler's reply. He said it was plain nonsense for a conductor to "decide to do much" or "decide to do little," that he should simply be natural and do however much or little the character of the music required. Convincing, but perhaps one ought to make certain allowances. When Furtwängler, at the height of his fame, conducted the Vienna or Berlin Philharmonic, he presided in each case a group of excellent musicians who knew the standard classical works superbly well and who were intimately familiar with his very personal way of conducting them. Under the circumstances he knew that only a minimum was needed from him to warrant a clean technical execution, and that therefore practically his entire effort, physical and otherwise, could be devoted to producing exactly the kind of music that he wanted. This is a near-ideal situation. In conducting a contemporary work or a difficult work not as well known to the orchestra, a great deal more technical orientation may be necessary, and therefore the high or low emotional temperature of the music is no longer the only deciding factor. The situation becomes even more complex when the orchestra is of inferior quality and depends to a much greater degree on the conductor's continuous guidance and support in matters of rhythm and dynamics. An amount of movement that is perfectly adequate in conducting the Boston Symphony is likely to be woefully insufficient when the orchestra is the Podunk Philharmonic. A modern piece with many meter changes, played by an orchestra not in the top dozen, will demand from the conductor an explicitness of time beating patterns that would seem ludicrous in a Haydn symphony. Other circumstances that affect the situation are the acoustics of the hall and the seating arrangement of the musicians. And since the familiarity of the players with the music is such a determinant, most conductors will find that from the first rehearsal to the performance they may steadily decrease the amount of physical movement, particularly scholastic time-beating.

The inexperienced conductor will understand the problems much better when he tries to realize the exact predicament of the musician: he must read the music and at the same time watch the conductor, which means that under ordinary circumstances the conductor's gestures will be observed by the musician's peripheral vision only. The question is how much peripheral vision can be made available. This will depend on the musician's technical skill, orchestral experience and familiarity with the music — also on the complexity of the musical patterns to be read. It is approximately the same problem that the driver of a car faces in reading road signs. If he is an experienced, relaxed driver, he will not only see and read all the signs, but he will also make mental notes of shopwindows, of people on the sidewalks and many other details. On the other hand the inexperienced or nervous driver will be so busy with the operation of the vehicle that his peripheral vision will not take in more than the signs printed in very large letters. By the same token the musician whose entire attention is absorbed in deciding whether the next note is B♮ or B♭ will be unable to follow subtle changes in the beat, and he will clamor for a larger one. But give the same large beat to a musician who knows the piece practically from memory, and he will feel insulted.

Yet in addition to all this, musicians are not untouched by human frailties. They play not merely as well as they are able to, but as well as they want to play. Therefore a factor that will always register is the respect that they feel for their leader. When an internationally famous man appears on the podium, their attention is usually heightened to a degree that would be unthinkable in the case of even a highly-talented beginner. Richard Strauss in conducting the Vienna Philharmonic could depend on such limitless veneration from the musicians that he accomplished miraculous results with an all but invisible beat. Fritz Reiner, one of his disciples, used a similar technique with many American orchestras. And although he never seemed to have any difficulty in getting his ideas across, there appeared to be an occasional concern over the fact that his conducting amounted to a virtual suppression of kinetic energy. It was certainly not what Furtwängler had in mind when he asked for "whatever the music required." A colleague whom I saw once after he had just attended one of Reiner's concerts in Chicago confided to me that he had left during intermission, not because it was not good, but because it caused him physical agony to hear an orchestra play the most rousing fortissimos to a conductor's beat that never exceeded a radius of three inches. Physical restraint, yes, but perhaps this was too much of a good thing!

No reasonable person would ever doubt that Reiner's technique during the last years of his life was that of a mature master who knew superbly well how to achieve the exact effect that he wanted. But what made his beat so frustratingly inimitable and unlearnable was the fact that even the faintest suggestion of "dancing" the music had been forcibly removed from it. What Reiner used was a complicated and often unnatural set of symbols (a short, muscular staccato beat to express a broad, sweeping legato!) to which first rate musicians were able to react marvelously well; others would have been at a loss. The conductor who, in the beginning of his career, is still groping to establish an artistic personality and a clear physical presentation should realize for his own good that such an approach had better be left alone, and that generally the imitation of highly individualistic beating patterns (Furtwängler, Koussevitzky, Bernstein) is bound to be fruitless. If he is willing to follow the book — or a more conventional pattern — then he may have a far better chance to shape his artistic ideas so that they can be absorbed by the musicians, and that consequently he will be able to make music according to his inner vision. Conducting an orchestra is difficult enough, particularly if one wishes to adhere to a dignified and acceptable physical pattern, so that the seeking out of additional hurdles, such as the imitation of extreme time-beating patterns, appears to be an uncalled-for luxury.

Chapter 6:
The Performance.

A symphony concert is always a great event for the conductor. Even in the seasoned practitioner, who has conducted in public many hundreds of times, the confrontation with an audience brings about a state of heightened consciousness, a kind of euphoria. Part of this feeling is expressed in the thought that "everything that I am going to do during the next two hours is *very* important!" Basically it is the outgrowth of a deep sense of responsibility, but it is joyful at the same time. What irony when you hear some not very sophisticated concertgoer say, "He just stands up there waving his arms. What is so significant about that? This fine orchestra could probably get along without him!" How ludicrously naïve this statement appears by comparison with what the conductor himself experiences while standing on the podium! The state of concentration which the conducting of a major symphonic work requires is so intense that no one who has not personally experienced it can ever understand the sensation. Conducting Beethoven's Ninth Symphony, for instance, can give one the feeling of having spent an entire year of his life in one hour and ten minutes.

What is the reason for this intense concentration and for such a tremendous sense of responsibility? It has been said on occasion that in a symphony concert the orchestra ought to be so well rehearsed that the conductor's presence during performance should be almost unnecessary. To the initiated this is patent nonsense. No matter how clearly the rendition of the music may have been defined in rehearsal, no matter how carefully polished, in performance it is the conductor who supplies the spark that creates the essential excitement, and that accounts for the difference between inspiration and pedestrianism. How significant this spark should be will largely depend on the conductor's personality. One conductor will give everything he has to give during rehearsal. He will prepare his concert down to the smallest expressive detail, including the fullest extent of all the emotional peaks, so that the concert will essentially be an exact repetition of the dress rehearsal. Another will rehearse the orchestra most meticulously, but will quite purposely limit the giving of emotional resources, in order to have an element of surprise left in performance. Jean Martinon says that "the conductor should not *sell* his possibilities too early. He should prepare the orchestra technically, but keep a reserve which comes out only at the concert." Similarly, it is said of Gustav Mahler that in spite of the most painstaking preparation he always left an element of improvisation for the performance and thereby assured a spontaneous response from the orchestra which otherwise might not have been forthcoming. Sixten Ehrling, representing the opposite viewpoint — and he certainly does not stand alone — feels that "once the conductor has rehearsed

68

the orchestra in a certain way he should not change during the concert since this may make the musicians nervous and work to the detriment of the performance."

But whatever the merit of the viewpoints in this highly personal controversy may be, neither viewpoint could remotely be used to downgrade the conductor's presence during the concert. For even if he rehearses everything and leaves nothing to chance, he must furnish the final impulse that turns his rehearsal instructions into a sounding reality. He must minutely control each tempo or change of tempo, and he must provide animation here and restraint there. In short, rehearsing with an orchestra does not mean that you polish every detail and put it away in a drawer so that it will emerge life-size at the touch of a button. A certain amount of cleaning up that is done in rehearsal will show beneficially in performance no matter who conducts, but the major portion is only of value in relation to the conductor who is responsible for it and will not come to fruition in strange hands. Junior conductors in opera who occasionally must take over someone else's performance without a rehearsal know this only too well. In fact, the take-over conductor in opera has two choices open to him: he may follow the interpretation of the man who preceded him to the minutest detail (which is only possible if he has had the opportunity to observe his predecessor's performance), in which case he must sacrifice his own interpretative ideas and become a puppet, so to speak; or he may be bold and largely follow his own ideas, in which case he will risk many technical slips and an often inadequate response from the orchestra.

To the average layman in the audience it may appear that the main justification for the conductor's presence is "to hold things together," to see to it that all come in at the same time and keep the same tempo. Actually, with an orchestra of professional standing, this is his least challenging assignment and the one in which he could be most easily replaced. It is easy for a good concertmaster to start a new tempo by signaling with his bow, just as it is done in chamber music. He can keep things going in a neat fashion once the orchestra is well rehearsed. What he cannot do is to infuse life into the playing, to establish a clear musical meaning through a thousand detailed operations and to balance the various aspects of sound against each other.

Many years ago I attended a performance given by a much touted conductorless orchestra. It was a Classical size symphony orchestra, much larger than any of the conductorless chamber ensembles that have become so popular during the past few years. The performance, which reportedly had been preceded by thirty-six rehearsals, was extremely neat and refined and also utterly bland and impersonal. My reaction even then was that if it took six times as many rehearsals to do a concert without a conductor as it would have taken to do it with one, then it should have been six times as good — which was hardly the case! Musicians do not usually hate the conductor with such a passion that a mammoth effort of this kind would seem warranted for the sheer pleasure of getting rid of him.

Once we understand that the conductor is not merely a glorified traffic cop who keeps collisions from occurring but a planner and coordinator capable of making ninety different musical temperaments fuse their energies to serve a single artistic purpose, then we can also see why he must possess such a keen sense of responsibility. The slightest slip of concentration on his part can ruin a performance, not necessarily in the sense of bringing it to a dead stop, but by disturbing the delicate balance which is the essence of any artistically viable interpretation. The parts of a symphonic performance fit together like the pieces of a jigsaw puzzle: you cannot change one element without causing a dozen others to be displaced as a consequence. If, for instance, I make a bigger retard before a fermata than I had planned and rehearsed, this may mean that the fermata itself must be longer. It may also mean — in certain cases — that the section following the fermata must be started at a more deliberate pace. Ignoring these postulates may cause the performance to lose logic and cohesion and may give it an air of mediocrity.

Obviously, the conductor must be extremely convincing in all his actions during performance. He cannot take the attitude of saying, "Gentlemen, we have rehearsed all this very carefully, now it is up to you to make music." Nothing is up to them unless they feel his guiding hand and his invigorating inspiration at all times. Even the conductor who is a superb pedagogue and a master of rehearsal technique cannot hope for a good concert if he becomes a nonentity in the presence of an audience. And furthermore, he must establish a definite quality of consistency between rehearsals and performance. If he is an improviser in the sense of Mahler (or Martinon), he may well take a certain virtuoso passage faster in the concert than in any of the rehearsals. The musicians, if they respect him, will understand that this is an act of calculated bravado and follow him willingly. But if he gives them the impression that he is taking it faster because he cannot remember his original tempo or because he is nervous, then they will resent it, and the result may be nothing short of disastrous.

This brings us to the problem of emotional control while performing, the coping with a phenomenon often referred to as stage fright. The havoc that one's nerves can play with the rendition of a musical work must not be overlooked. A student who fails an exam will often say, "I cannot understand why I could not answer these questions. Yesterday I knew the answers perfectly!" There are many conductors who "yesterday knew the answers perfectly" but who nevertheless fail in performance. Strictly speaking, conducting should be much less subject to nerves than the playing of an instrument in public, for it is largely free of physical hazards. A pianist's work will be ruined if his fingers slip on the keys. A conductor, even in great nervous agitation, is not likely to reach a state where his normally clear beat becomes unclear. Of course, the baton in his hand may tremble a bit, but this is not a very serious contingency. Much more to be feared is the impact of nervousness on a psychological level where it interferes with the ability to find and maintain the correct tempo or to impart the proper feeling to the music. Here one should face the issue squarely and try to find the solution best suited to his own personality.

Carl Friedberg, the famous piano pedagogue, once wrote an article in which he stated categorically that stage fright was an expression of insecurity and that the artist who was fully in command of his assignment was not subject to it. Many performers would take violent issue with this statement, and actually it seems to miss a very essential point: when a violinist who knows that he has severe intonation problems in the cadenza of a concerto shows anxiety before going on the stage, this is not exactly stage fright, for it is the rational fear of a real danger. The depressing circumstance about most cases of stage fright is that they are at least partially irrational. Real stage fright is the anxiety shown by the violinist who is supremely sure of his intonation, a fear that he might perhaps drop his bow in the middle of a passage, or that a string might slip, or that he might forget to enter for an important solo, or fear of nothing in particular — just general anxiety. In the case of a conductor the situation is even more clearly recognizable: if he knows that his rehearsal time has been insufficient and that certain technical problems in the pieces on his program are beyond the capability of the orchestra, he may be forgiven for being fearful. But if the rehearsing period has been adequate, the orchestra is technically capable, he himself is fully confident as to the correctness of his interpretations, his scores are perfectly memorized, and still his knees are shaking, then his difficulty may be of a more serious nature.

It is, of course, impossible within the scope of these pages to deal with the problem in depth, but perhaps at least one helpful hint can be given. Every artist suffering from stage fright knows that he should try to suppress it or get rid of it, but that is essentially no help, just as it is of little avail if one tells a stutterer that he should try not to stutter. However, in stage fright, whatever its deeper psychological roots may be, the essential difficulty is an exaggerated concern over one's own ego and its confrontation with the outside world. The stage fright sufferer says to himself, consciously or subconsciously, "What will it do to my ego if this or that or the other happens to me while I am on stage?" Since one cannot simply eradicate these negative thoughts from the psyche, it seems most practical to displace them by another thought that will absorb all the attention. Logically, this can only be the impersonal concern with the work one performs. After all, as conductors we do not work for ourselves, we work for the composer. Therefore, trite as this may sound, humility is the cure of many psychological ills. If the conductor who performs Beethoven will give every iota of his attention to Beethoven and to the work and none to himself, he may thereby not only control his stage fright, but in addition offer a far better performance.

Since conducting is a very strenuous activity both physically and mentally, it is very important that the performance be approached in the best physical and mental condition. José Ferrer, in an article on acting, expresses the thought that the actor goes on stage to perform "should feel like a million dollars." This is of course equally true of a conductor, and Ferrer's suggestion to sleep for several hours before the performance will be just as beneficial to him as it is to the actor. Body and mind should be completely relaxed before a performance, and sleep can accomplish this better than anything else. The other requirement is a joyful state of mind. Arguments and unpleasantness before a concert should be avoided at all costs. I know of one case where a conductor canceled his appearance because on the way to the concert he had gotten into a violent argument with a police officer over a parking space for his automobile. This may be drastic, but it is understandable. A good orchestra manager knows this, and he will do his utmost to shield the conductor against all possible inconveniences and aggravations before the concert.

About the intake of food before performing the opinions vary greatly. One maestro must eat a steak before going on. He feels that nothing else will give him the necessary strength. Another will abhor the thought of substantial food prior to his appearance and only eat very lightly. However, most will agree that the intake of liquids before conducting should be carefully limited.

Before getting dressed, a hot shower followed by a vigorous spray of cold water can be very stimulating. If a conductor suffers from excessive perspiration — and most of them do — he may find salt tablets taken before the concert and perhaps during intermission a harmless and efficient remedy. They are available in every drugstore under various brand names, and not only have I found that they tend to reduce perspiration, but they will also counteract exhaustion. However, in taking them, the instructions should be followed meticulously, otherwise they may cause some discomfort.

What happens during the last hour preceding the beginning of the concert is very vital, particularly for the conductor who conducts without scores. This is the transitional period from the complete relaxation of sleep and eating to the complete concentration necessary to conduct the concert. It is essential to avoid unnecessary distractions during that hour. One should keep conversations to a minimum and try to be alone as much as possible. Of course, the conductor may find it advisable to establish a little personal contact with the members of the orchestra, perhaps greet them and wish them luck, perhaps give a few last minute instructions to the musicians — ("watch me for your entrance in the six-eight time" — "take your time on the solo, I'll follow you"), etc. Especially in less than top-ranking orchestras this will create a very pleasant (but not chummy!) atmosphere, and it will give the musicians the feeling that they are treated as human beings and not just as parts of a machine. But all this should be very brief and to the point. Jokes or anecdotes are neither necessary nor appropriate at that time. In fact, it is hard to conceive how a conductor can tell an off-color joke to a group of musicians and then go out on stage to conduct Beethoven's Fifth Symphony! He should use as much time as he can to put himself in the right mood for the *holy office* — I am using these words advisedly — of presiding over a symphonic performance. Thus he may find it desirable to go over the works in his mind for a last time or perhaps take a quick look at the printed text in order to clarify some remaining ambiguities.

When at last the lights are lowered and the conductor enters the stage, he should feel in his whole body that he is in the limelight and that whatever he does now is of the utmost significance. There is no need to make an old-fashioned, melodramatic entrance. But it is also not recommended to underplay the appearance by being either apologetic or overly businesslike. Perhaps this somewhat unorthodox analogy may be pardoned: when the priest steps to the altar, he does not act as if he were God, but he acts with the full consciousness of being the spokesman of God. Similarly, the conductor need not be arrogant to know that at the moment of his entrance he is the center of attention. Therefore he should not race out at the first dimming of the lights as if he wanted to catch a train. He should wait until the lights are fully dimmed, then give the audience an opportunity to enjoy — yes, enjoy! — a few seconds of complete silence. After that he will walk on stage in an erect and dignified fashion and acknowledge briefly but graciously the applause that will presumably receive him. Some conductors demand that the musicians stand up at their entrance. I find this somewhat unnecessary and in some cases outright embarrassing, except when it is a spontaneous and unrehearsed gesture which the orchestra renders out of respect for the leader's personality — certainly not a routine occurrence! There is one rather nice if possibly old-fashioned custom that I like to adhere to: to bow to the orchestra first, and then to the audience. This the musicians will appreciate, and such a small courtesy may easily inspire them to perform with a greater amount of enthusiasm.

Psychologically speaking, the following few seconds, could be the most important ones of the entire evening. This is when the proper mood for the concert must be established. Nothing could be more repugnant than a conductor who at this moment strikes a bold, dramatic pose for the benefit of the audience ("isn't he handsome!"), as if to say, "Be sure and watch me now; you have never seen anyone so terrific!" There is no denying that a certain dramatic quality is inherent in the activity of conducting an orchestra, but the drama should emerge as the result of projecting musical intensity, not as something planned and planted outside and away from the music! The really sincere conductor will, of course, focus on the orchestra and not on the audience, and most of all away from his own personality! He may seem to say to the musicians, "This is our great moment: now we shall make beautiful music together!" Such an attitude will appear almost automatically if the conductor, rather than worrying about his effect on the audience, will concentrate completely on the intended sound of the first measures of music he is about to conduct. At this time any conscious concern over his appearance should be unnecessary. If he has trained himself to stand straight and to make clear and harmonious gestures, then the joy of making music expressed by every muscle in his body will easily and effortlessly reach the listeners and affect them in a most positive fashion!

Not much can be said about the actual performance that has not been said already. Hopefully, the rehearsal work has achieved its purpose, and conductor and orchestra members are confidently looking forward to a good concert. Now the conductor's task is to keep things technically well under control, to indicate the correct tempi and tempo changes, to maintain the proper balance by making adjustments where they are needed, to give the necessary cues, and most of all, to furnish the inspiration through gestures and expressions that will draw the best efforts from the musicians. The main factor that distinguishes the performance from every rehearsal is that now *all* the conductor's actions must point in a positive direction: if a solo is played very beautifully he should definitely acknowledge it with a smile, but in the opposite case he must strenuously refrain from showing any signs of disapproval, since this might create resentment and affect the remainder of the performance adversely. In essence this is a question of good manners. Even more important is that if a bad mishap occurs in performance, the conductor must not let it upset his own state of mind. If he should get angry because the first trombonist came in a beat too soon, his own concentration will undoubtedly suffer, and a few seconds later he himself may make a stupid mistake! In conducting there is no crying over spilled milk: if the first movement of a symphony was bad, the second, third and fourth can still be heavenly, provided that the conductor shows the right spirit by concentrating his energy on what is to come and by deliberately driving from his mind all thoughts of earlier mishaps.

Some time after the first five or ten minutes of the concert, the conductor, if he is sensitive, will know how the performance is being received by the audience. Without interrupting his stream of concentration he will become alert to the little signals that are sent in his direction from behind, and he will not have to wait for the applause to know how "they" like it. An audience that is held spellbound by the music keeps quiet. If there is a continuous rustling of programs, and if the sneezes and coughs remind one of a ward for upper respiratory diseases, then chances are that the message of the music is not reaching them. It is hard to say whether in such a case the conductor has any effective means at his command to remedy the situation. Perhaps the mood of the audience indicates that his interpretations are shallow or pedestrian, or that the orchestra is insufficiently rehearsed. The best he can do is not to let the restlessness bewilder him and to concentrate even harder on the task of projecting the music. Possibly his efforts will be rewarded, and the reaction will improve as the performance continues.

Admittedly or not, the most beautiful sound in the conductor's ears is the applause that greets the end of a piece. From its spontaneity and intensity he can easily tell what impression the music has made. But even though we all want to be liked, one should keep in mind the fact that it is not the conductor's only duty to draw applause. For there is more that gives a clue as to the quality of music making than the volume and duration of the handclapping or the number of bravos heard. Obviously, a mediocre performance of Tchaikovsky's Fifth will draw more applause than a superb one of Mahler's Fourth. But this is no reason not to perform Mahler's Fourth, nor will it suggest to the sensitive baton wielder that he should spend his entire career conducting pieces whose rousing endings excite the lay listener and prepare the ground for an ovation! Any audience reaction must be interpreted in relation to the piece performed, and in the case of some pieces of music, a subdued reaction is quite normal. I have always felt —

especially with some difficult works — that the greatest compliment for conductor and performers is not an immediate salvo of applause, but a spellbound silence of several seconds at the end of the piece, with the applause bursting forth afterwards.

In acknowledging the audience's reaction it is customary in this country to have the whole orchestra rise immediately after the end of the piece. What happens after that — the alternation of solo bows by the conductor and invitations to the orchestra to rise — is a well known routine that need not be discussed here. But there are a few points that deserve to be mentioned. An actor taking his curtain call at the end of a dramatic performance is always told to "bow in character," so that the audience will not be jolted out of the mood of the play. One feels tempted to recommend the same to the man with the baton if he is not sensitive enough to do it instinctively. There is nothing more offensive and disillusioning than a conductor who, after the sublimely ethereal final chords of Mahler's *Lied von der Erde*, takes his bows with a broad grin on his face! Even the speed of the bows should not violate the mood of the music just concluded, otherwise it might appear that the conductor is an emotional faker and that his ostensible involvement with the music was merely switched on for effect.

The other important item is the advisability for the conductor to acknowledge important solos in orchestral works by asking the players to rise separately. A French hornist playing the difficult and exposed solo in the second movement of Tchaikovsky's Fifth or a flute player in Debussy's *L'après-midi d'un faune* is asked to do an outstanding bit of work, but he receives no additional pay for it. Therefore, the least the conductor can do if the solo was well played is to give that musician a solo bow. This is another small gesture which in the long run can become an important morale factor in the playing of the orchestra.

The fascinating and also dangerous aspect of any performance before an audience — and a symphony concert is no exception — is that one can never predict its outcome. The conductor may be very sure of himself, he may know that he has a capable and well rehearsed orchestra and that he is performing beautiful works of music, but he does not know whether the performance is going to have that added factor, that special magic which makes the difference between mere competence on one side and the ability to grip an audience on the other. It is a very intangible factor, to be sure. Sometimes the performance of a very outstanding vocal or instrumental soloist may produce it. The audience is so keyed up with keen anticipation that everyone expects it to happen, but by no means always. In a purely orchestral performance it would be reasonable to assume that a magic quality can only appear after all the technical hurdles have been taken, but this is not true. Often an extremely well drilled and fluent performance will glide along on wings of competence and nothing more. And sometimes one that is not so well drilled and fluent will suddenly strike gold.

Generally speaking, audiences are very sensitive to this phenomenon. In fact, they should be because they are part of it. This type of magic is started by the performers, but it will not get past the footlights unless the listeners are ready to receive it. For that reason we speak of a good or a bad audience. When you perform for people who are attending the concert because they feel that it will give them social status, then it may be difficult or impossible to reach them with a metaphysical message. Luckily, as a rule the sensitive listeners are, if not in a majority, at least in a strong enough minority to spark a powerful reaction where it is called for. Thus, a really beautiful presentation of music is not likely to miss completely in its audience reception, even with a so-called bad audience.

However, be the audiences good or bad, the conductor should be able to tell after a comparatively short time what the relationship between both sides of the footlights is going to be. On the other hand, the factor that defies all guessing is the reaction of the critics. This is a much discussed problem and often an unhappy one. Artists may try to discount the importance of newspaper reviews, but in their hearts they know that the few lines or paragraphs that will appear in the paper the following morning are their lifeline. Critics can destroy an artist, if they try long and hard enough, no matter how the audience may feel about him. Therefore every performer longs for good reviews in the paper — let him not tell you otherwise! Of course, the wise artist will take them in the proper spirit: he will be very happy over a good review on account of the practical advantages that it may give him, but he will not be swept off his feet in a false sense of personal glory. On the other hand, a bad review, though very annoying, should not deprive the performer of his self-confidence. Critics have to be taken with a grain of salt. It is just as wrong to take all their writings for pure coin as it is to declare haughtily that "they just don't know what they are talking about." Max Rudolf made a most interesting statement to me about this. "When someone says something bad about me," he said, "even though I may know that the person is an idiot, I do some soul-searching to find if there is not perhaps some small grain of truth in his words that might be helpful to me." And indeed, though many of our music critics have obtained their positions on very flimsy credentials, there are others whose erudition and sensitivity are unmistakable. Often the difficulty is not their ignorance — which is a possibility — but their surfeit with music and the necessity to listen to it in the best or the worst mood. Furthermore, even the best among them have little or big prejudices that will color their writings and occasionally cause them to evaluate an artist unjustly.

Some critics will always mirror the mood of the audience in their writings, others will try their utmost to appear in exact opposition to it. Some will judge a performance only in the most general terms, perhaps because they lack the erudition to do anything else. Others will take pleasure in puzzling the majority of their readers by their sophisticated discussion of technical details. What I frequently find disconcerting, even in intelligent critics, is that their appraisal of an orchestral performance, though undoubtedly sincere, may be diametrically opposed to the opinion of the conductor himself and of all the musicians. Sometimes you feel that you have really given your best in a concert and that this was amply reflected by the most enthusiastic audience reaction. The next day you read in the paper that the performance was stodgy and pedestrian. Or else, you walk off the stage feeling miserable about all the things that did not materialize the way you wanted them to, about the silly slips in various solo entrances, and about the general lack of inspiration. Yet the morning paper informs you glowingly that this was the most beautiful and gripping orchestral playing that has been heard in years!

Perhaps these psychological hazards make our profession more interesting and challenging. A conductor need not curse the critics nor heap imprecations upon the audience. His wisest policy is to give his very best effort on every occasion, to keep developing, and to make sure that each one of his performances is a little better than the one that preceded it. Everything else is a matter of luck, and since it cannot be influenced, it had best be accepted with the necessary amount of fatalism.

PART II:

PHYSICS AND METAPHYSICS.

Chapter 7:

A View from the Pit — Opera and Related Arts.

In the United States there is at present not much demand for conductors of full-fledged professional opera companies. In the first place, there are no more than half a dozen organizations that can truthfully be characterized as professional companies, and their conductors are more often than not either men of international reputation who are highly experienced practitioners of their art or at least men who know how to create an image of being highly knowledgeable and experienced. However, operas are performed in many places in America. Besides our professional companies there is a large number of civic opera companies, sometimes entirely staffed with local talent, sometimes with name singers as guest artists. Then there is an even larger number of opera workshops in colleges and universities. All these organiations need conductors. And the fact that the conducting of an opera is not taking place at the Metropolitan Opera does not make it any easier; in fact, it often makes it more difficult.

It is not at all uncommon in this country to find an opera production conducted by a man who is obviously unfamiliar with the medium, and who tries with greater or lesser success to adjust to its exigencies. This may be an uphill fight, for the fact is — without any ifs and buts — that the technical requirements of opera conducting are formidable. Although this should be self-evident, time and again we find a conductor who decides that if he is able to conduct a Tchaikovsky symphony he certainly ought to be able to conduct a Mozart opera, where the orchestra is only half as big. Needless to say, such an enthusiastic maestro may have second thoughts on the subject before his first rehearsal with the stage is half over! But then, when something goes wrong in an opera, one may always blame it on the unmusical singers, on the choristers who simply refuse to watch the conductor, on the incompetent stage director, on the bad lighting and many other factors. It would be much harder to alibi one's failure with a symphony orchestra by saying that the clarinetist played on the wrong instrument or that the timpanist forgot to tune his drums!

Some of the difficulties of this complex medium are quite obvious even to the layman. The opera conductor needs to control an apparatus that is very much spread out in space, often to such an extent that the comparatively slow speed with which the sound travels will play tricks: a singer, standing very far upstage, may be under the impression that he is accurately following the conductor's beat. And yet, the delay in the travel of sound will cause his entrance to sound late to conductor and audience. With a chorus this may become an even greater problem. In these cases it is the conductor's duty to insist on a slightly anticipated attack.

In a symphony orchestra all musicians, experienced or inexperienced, play from the printed music. Therefore the letter-perfect rendition is a matter of course, except in the case of outright incompetence. But even the least experienced

81

singer on an opera stage must sing his entire role from memory, and so the possibility of a poorly learned or poorly remembered musical detail is always there. Besides that, the opera singer must be a musician and an actor at the same time. Therefore, he cannot give more than half of his attention to musical matters, when sometimes all of it would barely be sufficient! Furthermore, musical ensembles are often sung by performers placed in different areas of the stage, and so far apart that they cannot hear each other. (For the sake of argument: how would the coordination be in a performance of Brahms' Double Concerto, if the violinist and the cellist were placed at different ends of the stage?)

An even more common problem is the inability of the singers to hear the orchestra, whose sound from the pit may not reach the stage too well. In fact, the unhappy truth of the matter is that the better a singer is able to hear the orchestra, the less will the audience be able to hear the singer. The sound of a well controlled orchestra playing from a low pit is very good for the total balance, but it may be almost inaudible to the singer on stage while he is singing, and thereby drive him to distraction.

Yet there are more technical problems that the opera conductor is faced with. His presence of mind must be phenomenal: he must always be able to improvise, for even in the best rehearsed opera performance surprises happen all the time. A singer who drives himself into an emotional frenzy at a climactic moment, even though he knows his music well, may understandably start a phrase two beats too soon or three beats too late. Such a mistake, which might cause an orchestral musician to lose his job, will in this case be accepted with an indulgent smile, and the conductor will have to make the adjustments. And, as if these hazards were not enough, opera performances are mostly underrehearsed. A symphony program, consisting of seventy-five minutes of playing time, will on the average rate four to five full rehearsals. An opera of three to four hours length may not even get that much, and only in rare cases more than that.

Let us take the case of the young maestro X.Y., who for several seasons has been the music director of a small town symphony orchestra. He is a capable musician, and he has done well with his group — he also has pleased the audiences. Now suddenly a local organization decides that it is time to present a home grown opera. Mozart's *Marriage of Figaro* (in English!) is chosen, and our local maestro is put in command. At first he is a bit awestruck: of course he has never conducted an opera in his life. In fact, not having spent much time in the big cities, he has attended no more than half a dozen live performances of operas, and *Figaro* was not one of them. Nevertheless he approaches his task like a trouper: he studies the score very carefully, listens to the available recordings, and reads many books on the subject. After several weeks of serious study he feels confident that he can handle the assignment.

Having come to the podium from the violin and not being a very adept performer on the piano, our young maestro had to depend on several assistants for the musical preparation of the singers and the chorus. However, he did not

82

take his task lightly and took musical charge of all the ensemble and staging rehearsals, with an assistant playing the piano. Up to this point everything went very well. In fact, the maestro was quite impressed with the musicianship of the solo singers, recruited through auditions among regional amateurs and college personnel, who had no trouble following his beat, even when they were not noticeably looking at him. After several piano rehearsals the tempi as well as details of dynamics and phrasing appeared precisely set and well drilled, and everyone seemed happy.

Then the maestro held two reading sessions with the orchestra alone. (He could not get the singers to attend these sessions, since the stage director felt that he needed the time with them.) There were some minor difficulties — the first oboist had to miss one rehearsal on account of illness, and the second horn player the other, but on the whole things went well. Everybody in the orchestra agreed that this was not too different from playing a Mozart symphony.

Now the time for the real test has come: the first rehearsal of solo singers, chorus and orchestra together. We have moved to the auditorium where the performance is to take place. It has no orchestra pit, therefore the orchestra sits on the same level with the audience. (The stage director, being aware of this shortcoming, has wisely placed a set of risers on the stage, so that the feet of the singers would not be covered by the heads of the orchestra musicians.) At the starting time of the rehearsal the curtain is already open, offering a rather bleak vista. The stage sets have not been finished yet, and so there are only a few props on the stage (dressing table, chair, armchair, etc.), but the room assigned by the count to Figaro and Susanna has no walls, allowing the spectator's eyes to gaze at the not very inspiring red brick wall of the auditorium. Under the circumstances it is only natural that no effort has been made to get the lighting ready. On the rehearsal schedule it had said "lights marked" — which in stage jargon means that a few spotlights may hit the stage, but always at the wrong time, in the wrong area, and with the wrong color and intensity.

The performers are all in place and it is time to start. Now the conductor begins with the overture. The orchestra is apparently quite well prepared, and there is not too much in the rendition that calls for extensive corrections. However, our maestro is a perfectionist, and so he repeats the opening in order to assure flawless synchronization between strings and first bassoon (the second bassonist had mercifully been advised not to play the passage!), and he also repeats the ending of the piece in order to improve the incisiveness of the staccato passage in the woodwinds.

Next is the first duet between Figaro and Susanna. The orchestral introduction goes passably well. Figaro rushes on the stage, trying to put himself into the lively mood of the scene. He measures the imaginary room with his yardstick and begins to sing, his back turned to the audience, as he had been instructed by the stage director. The conductor who cannot hear the singer's voice at all is about to interrupt, but then changes his mind. Knowing the bass-baritone to be a secure musician, he imagines that the cue was probably correctly sung. This proves to be true when the singer turns around — his lips are moving at the right time, and even a bare hint of vocal sound reaches the conductor's ears. Meanwhile Susanna has entered and is trying on her bonnet. A very spirited action develops between the two. Yet our maestro is getting more unhappy by the minute. He can only hear very little of the voices, and when he does hear them it is evident that the precision between singers and orchestra leaves something to be desired. When he notices that the singers seem to be running away from him, he speeds up the orchestra in order to catch up with them. This results in even greater confusion: the singers, having noticed his somewhat frantic movements, conclude that they must be singing too slowly and increase the speed even more. When the number comes to a close it is obvious to the conductor that he must interrupt.

The following dialogue ensues:

Conductor: My friends, you must try to follow me better. We were not together at all. Can't you look at me a little more? You always seem to turn away from me . . .

Figaro: Maestro, we are looking at you all we can, but we must act, too. Besides that, we cannot hear the orchestra very well.

Conductor: Nor can I hear you. Is this full voice? Can't you sing a little louder?

Susanna: I don't know about you (looking at her partner) but I am giving all I have. (Figaro nods affirmatively.) And while we are stopping, do you mind, maestro, taking the tempo a little faster? It seems to me that in piano rehearsal we were taking it twice as fast, and it is very hard to . . .

Conductor (interrupting her a trifle angrily): What do you mean, twice as fast? I am taking exactly the same tempo as in piano rehearsal. Well, we shall try it again.

Stage director (who has quietly approached the conductor from his station in the center of the auditorium, in a whisper): I am sorry to tell you I could not understand a single word. The orchestra is much too loud. Can't you make them play a little softer?

Conductor (with resignation): All right, all right . . .

So much suffering for only the first piece of the opera. Now let us try to look at the individual complaints a little more dispassionately. ("Objectively" is hardly the right word for one who is himself guilty of being a conductor!)

If our maestro had been more experienced, he would immediately have been alarmed when he did not hear Figaro's voice at his first entrance. Even with the singer's back turned to the audience, even with the absence of a sound-reflecting surface (the back wall of the stage set!) the conductor should still at least hear enough to be sure that the singer is singing. It is an almost inevitable conclusion that if the conductor cannot hear a singer, most of the audience cannot hear him either. So, at the first inkling of danger, the conductor's left, or "piano" hand should have gone up in a warning gesture to the musicians. If this is of no avail, the next step is to stop the orchestra and to ask the musicians to consider every forte in their parts a mezzo piano and every mezzo forte a pianissimo. This ought to do the trick, even under unfavorable circumstances, unless the voices are of inadequate volume, in which case there is no help. But here this was certainly not the case.

"Can't you look at me a little more?" It is the standard apprehension of all inexperienced opera conductors that the singers do not look at them enough. In fact, the beginner on the opera podium always feels ignored by the singers: He admonishes them to give him more direct eye contact for fear that otherwise the precision may suffer. Sometimes a very experienced conductor, if he is of the older school, will do the same, not out of fear but out of principle: he wishes to leave no doubt in the singers' minds as to who is in command. In between, there is a type of conductor who is experienced but more relaxed. He realizes that looking straight at the maestro's beat is not the only way to stay together with the orchestra; in fact, it is not even the best way. Singers should be trained from their early beginnings to *listen* to the orchestra. This will eliminate much of the need for continuous eye contact. Unfortunately many of our opera singers listen to the orchestra with only half an ear since looking at the conductor has become such a comfortable crutch to them. When they begin to force themselves to look less and listen more, they will not only find this the safer method, but they will also please the stage director (and themselves and the audience) by looking more like live human beings on stage and less like automatic puppets led on strings by the conductor.

"You were taking the tempo twice as fast as in rehearsal." Let us for the time being ignore the word "twice." Opera singers are not generally in the habit of checking tempi with the metronome, and they are also often given to dramatic exaggerations. So we shall just assume that the complaint alleges a discrepancy of temporarily undetermined extent between the tempi of piano and orchestra rehearsals. We shall not immediately absolve our maestro of all guilt. Not being the most seasoned practitioner of the baton, it is quite possible that he did not assert his own will very firmly but gave in to the resistance of some of the technically weaker players. This is quite likely to happen in the case of some of the second violin figurations in the first duet in *Figaro*: not that they are outlandishly difficult, but they are a little easier to play at a more moderate speed, and the natural instinct of the weaker player is to slow down. But let us also look at the other side of the coin. It takes a very experienced opera singer to judge a tempo correctly. The less experienced one has a tendency to judge it not with his mind but with his lungs and vocal cords. What happens very often is that a singer has sung most of the piano rehearsals in half voice, which means that everything could be taken fast or slow with no particular difficulty. The voice given at half volume makes no physical demands! Then there is the orchestra rehearsal sung in full voice. This takes a lot more breath, and all of a sudden there does not seem to be enough wind to sustain the long phrases. Rationalization of the singer: I do not seem to have enough breath to sustain a vocal line that has never given me trouble before; obviously the tempo must be slower!

This is a phenomenon worth looking into for every opera singer. We may tell a singer a hundred times to "sing naturally," to give no more on stage than he would in a room. Yet plainly this is an unrealistic request. A singer always gives more voice on stage with an orchestra than he does in a room without one, even though he may not admit it. More likely than not this will also influence his feeling about the speed of the music. And since the idea that he needs so much more breath to sing with an orchestra is an unflattering one to him, he takes the easy way out and blames it all on the tempo!

What is the remedy in this problematical situation? It all depends on the circumstances. Generally speaking, natural musicianship and an inborn sense of tempo on the part of the singer (and, needless to say, of the conductor) plus a certain amount of experience on both sides of the footlights are the best safeguards against such incidents. Even so the conductor should not leave matters to chance. He should insist on a number of rehearsals on the stage, with the piano in the pit, and he should conduct at least part of these rehearsals. It may seem foolish to wield a baton over two singers and a humble pianist, but the advantages of this procedure by far outweigh its apparent silliness. In these piano rehearsals the conductor should from time to time ask the singers to sing in their full voices. This will give them at least an approximate idea of how much carrying power they need in order to "subsist" vocally in the large auditorium. It will also give the conductor an approximate idea of what he is to expect in the way of irregularities of tempo on the part of the singers. This method may not be a cure-all, but it will certainly prevent some of the crises in orchestra rehearsal from occurring.

Let us now look at the stage director's complaint that he could not understand the words. In moments of complete despair concerning this problem every participant in an opera production may remember that it is always easier to understand the words in a hall filled with people than in an empty house. However, I am offering this point only as a final consolation. It is certainly not an invitation to ignore the problem! This must be faced in its proper extent, which may take a certain amount of courage. Naturally, a great deal depends on the size and volume of the singing voice, which is not to say that large voices always produce good diction or vice versa. In fact, quite often the opposite is true. It means only that the larger voice, if treated properly in every other respect, has a better opportunity of getting the words across to the audience. Within that basic reality much depends on how the voice is produced. Some voices are produced in such a fashion that the projection of words is no problem; with some others it never ceases to be a problem. To begin with, there are people who pronounce clearly when they speak and others who do not. Unfortunately, not too many voice teachers fully realize the importance of this point. If they did, and if they tried to correct bad diction most vigorously from the very beginning, then a great deal of later trouble might be averted. However, in this country so much emphasis is placed on the studying of correct diction in two or three foreign languages (with greatly varying degrees of success!) that English diction often becomes the stepchild. Add to this the often encountered attitude of young singers that says:

86

"Why should I worry about pronouncing a language that I have spoken all my life?" — it is hard to think of a sillier statement, for speaking English and singing in English are two entirely different things! — and you will understand at least part of the trouble. Furthermore, voice teachers often spend most of their time making their students produce the correct vowels since it is mostly the vowel that is responsible for the beauty of the tone. On the other hand, it is mostly the consonant that is responsible for the clarity of the diction. I have also found that many voice teachers tend to confuse the elements of duration and intensity in the pronunciation of consonants. They are afraid of intensely pronounced consonants for fear of producing what is referred to as a "choppy" vocal line, when in reality it is not the intensity but the exaggerated duration of the consonants that cause the trouble and makes the line appear "choppy."

It should be understood that there is a basic contradiction in the two factors controlling vocal delivery that causes most of our diction problems: the vowel, or singing tone (which for our purposes are one and the same thing), can be produced in various places within the available resonance facilities without losing its carrying power. In fact, a tone that is produced "farther back in the mouth" (to use the elusive imagery common with voice teachers) has a better chance not only of being heard but of sounding fuller and richer than one that is produced "in a shallow fashion," meaning in the area of the lips and the tip of the tongue. On the other hand the consonant that is *not* produced in this "shallow" area of the tip of the tongue and the lips is almost completely worthless. It cannot be heard beyond a very short distance! It therefore behooves the singer to achieve a compromise between "full-throated" vocalism and "forward" production of consonants, and for some singers this is unfortunately an almost insoluble problem.

It is advisable for every opera conductor to be familiar with these basic facts. Otherwise telling a singer to "pronounce more clearly" may be of no more avail than to tell a string player not to scratch.

But there is still more to our problem. Richard Strauss states very interestingly that in listening to the dress rehearsal of an opera in the morning and to the performance the same evening, one may observe that the diction is ever so much clearer during dress rehearsal. Why? The singers obviously do not wish to "waste" their voices in dress rehearsal, with a performance only a few hours away, therefore they "save" vocally, which enables them to concentrate a great deal more on the clarity of the diction. One might say they will not let the vocal production get in the way of the pronunciation. During performance, on the other hand, their prime concern is the vocal sound ("that is what you get paid for!"), and unless experience has taught them how to attend to both factors at once, they may easily tend to neglect the diction unduly.

But let us return to our opera rehearsal. After the first crisis things took a turn for the better. The knowledge that a certain problem exists sometimes almost provides a solution. And so our singers have tried their best to "project words," to "watch the beat," and conductor and orchestra on their part have made great additional efforts not to drown out the vocal sounds from the stage. The improvement was soon noticeable. (Perhaps it will strike some readers as strange that one should fear the danger of drowning out the singers with the spare and elegant sounds of a Mozart orchestra, but believe me, it is possible! In correcting this imbalance, the conductor will first turn his attention to the sustained notes in horns and bassoons: they should almost automatically be played a degree softer than indicated. The other likely sources of trouble are sustained notes in the other winds and then in the lower strings. Quick figurations will seldom drown out a singer, only sustained sounds.)

The next difficulty occurred in Bartolo's D Major aria: it was started at a briskly paced Allegro con brio, as called for by the composer. But when the singer arrived at the quick parlando in triplet rhythm, he could no longer maintain the pace. However, the conductor rigidly adhered to the tempo of the beginning, and soon both were moving in different directions.

Dialogue, after interruption by the conductor:

Bartolo: Maestro, I am sorry, this is too fast for me. I cannot possibly sing the triplets that fast.

Conductor: What do you mean, "that fast"? This is the tempo you yourself started. You don't expect me to change tempo in the middle of a Mozart allegro, do you?

Bartolo: Maestro, I am not trying to tell you what to do. Only I know that I need more time to pronounce the words. After all, I have a voice to contend with. You cannot ignore that and treat me as if I were a bassoon player!

Again, with more experience and insight this nasty little exchange could have been avoided. Perhaps the bass did start the aria a bit too fast (it is an unfortunate but common weakness of many musicians to take a tempo faster when there are no technical difficulties.) On the other hand the conductor should not have acted so righteously about "not changing the tempo in the middle of a Mozart allegro." Mozart, along with most other composers, certainly did not expect his performers to be machines. A small modification of the tempo is always permissible, particularly when it is done for a good purpose, such as making the words of a certain passage intelligible. The important thing is to do it so gently that the audience does not become aware of the change. As Jonel Perlea once said to me: "What really matters in opera is not to maintain a rigid tempo, but to return to the correct tempo after each slight compromise that has been made for the sake of a singer."

In this special case it would have been wise for the conductor to use the measure before the triplets begin in the orchestra for an ever so slight deceleration. This is not only practical, it is also done for psychological effect: the singer, in starting the triplets, notices immediately how comfortable it is to sing them at the pace prepared by the conductor. He may then either continue at exactly the prepared speed, which is unobjectionable since the deceleration was only minute. Or else his ambition may be aroused ("I don't want to be babied. I can sing this faster!") and thus he may return to the original speed, which is even better, provided that the conductor is ready to follow. Sometimes the advantage of a concession made by the conductor to the singer lies not just in the temporary comfort that it gives the singer but in the improved psychological relationship between singer and conductor, which in turn makes the singer more willing to compromise on his part when necessary. We are here speaking in terms of imperceptible changes of tempo — nothing that could ruin the structure of a musical line. However, to the singer they are perceptible enough to make all the difference between vocal comfort and discomfort. Of course this must not be overdone. We feel very little respect for the routinier-conductor, whose sole claim to fame consists of being the "perfect accompanist": he can and does follow the singer smoothly through every excess of bad taste, and what happens to the structure of the music is of precious little concern to him. The really skillful conductor, the one who possesses artistic integrity, is not prepared to give up his scepter to a vocalist. He does not just follow blindly but has everything carefully planned. But he realizes that the singer can only perform well when he is comfortable. Thus he makes reasonable concessions in order to be able to exact reasonable concessions. Most of all, the opera conductor worthy of the name must "breathe with the singer" — not literally, of course — but he must be able to feel where the singer needs an ever so small amount of additional time in order to negotiate a phrase calmly and securely rather than laboriously.

We shall not recount here all the ups and downs which our young maestro encountered during his first full rehearsal of opera. But it may be worth narrating what happened in the first encounter between chorus and orchestra, the G Major allegro in 6/8 time. Here the conductor led the orchestral introduction at a rather moderate speed, making it possible for the first violins to give the proper articulation to each sixteenth-note. Perhaps he had forgotten how the chorus had sung this during preliminary rehearsals, perhaps he did not care. Anyway, the choristers apparently remained unimpressed with the tempo of the introduction and came in at a much faster speed, the one that had been drilled into them earlier. The conductor tried to restrain them, but it was hopeless, and after a few measures there was such confusion that he had to stop. What followed were the usual recriminations: "why don't you watch my beat?," "you took it much faster in piano rehearsal," etc. Finally, with the helpful mediation of the chorus director, a compromise was reached, and when the piece was repeated, everything went according to plan.

Again, experience might have helped to alleviate the situation. To work with an opera chorus effectively you need patience, but you also need some psychological understanding. The chorister is very different in his psychic makeup from the solo singer. He is not an "artist" in the same sense (choristers, please spare my life, this is not meant as an insult!). He knows that no matter how well he as an individual may sing, the effect of his contribution on the total of the performance is small. Therefore, his personal ambition is understandably limited. His responsi-

89

bility consists of performing in an efficient manner the things that have been drilled into him. Thus, he is the closest approximation to a performing machine. Woe to the conductor who freely changes tempi with a chorus. It always leads to disaster! Choristers have a collective memory for tempi which is usually quite reliable. And they use it to the hilt: they simply will not modify a tempo once they have learned it in grueling hours of chorus rehearsal with piano. They can actually look at a conductor and not see him; that is, they see him, of course, but they take no notice if what he demands tends to contradict their earlier efforts. If a chorister says of a conductor that he has "a good beat," what he really means is that he takes each tempo with full conviction in accordance with the earlier preparation by the chorus master.

However, for the adventurous opera conductor there are ways of influencing the speed of a chorus from the pit. I discovered this quite by accident, and rather than jealously guard my secret, I shall communicate it here for whatever it may be worth. When I once had difficulties in coordinating the tempo of the chorus with that of the orchestra, I started instinctively to mouth the chorus words while conducting. (This is something which in the case of solo singers is anathema to most serious conductors. Weingartner used to say: "I am a conductor — not a prompter!") My mouthing the words of the chorus proved extremely helpful though, and the resulting coordination was nearly perfect. However, it necessitated my memorizing all the words of the chorus, which in some operas could be quite a chore. So the next time a similar situation arose, I mouthed the words again. But since that time I had not memorized them I had to mouth other words — any words that came to my mind. In fact, I blush to confess that sometimes I mouthed words that are not quotable in decent company. But apparently the trick worked: the choristers, unaware of what I was pronouncing, simply succumbed to the suggestive power of this device and followed me like lambs to the slaughter. I have used the same trick many times since then when I felt that it was needed. It may not work in all such cases, but it has worked well for me.

Perhaps something should be said here about the technique of accompanying dancers, although this may be treading on dangerous ground. Ballet dancers (and they are the only variety used in opera) as a rule are even more "drilled" than choristers, but their sense of tempo is often far less reliable and far more dependent on external circumstances, such as the floor they dance on, the weight of their costumes, their state of physical tiredness, etc. At the same time many ballet dancers tend to be very much on the defensive when the slightest hint is made to impugn their musicianship. Often they act as if they had built-in metronomes! So when a ballerina stops in the middle of her big solo during orchestra rehearsal and wails at the conductor: "but, maestro, you took it *three* times as fast yesterday!" he should not take the time to explain to the lady what it would actually mean to take a tempo *three* times as fast! He should merely smile graciously, start the dance once again, and this time take it *a shade* faster.

In conducting for a ballet you are often told to watch the feet of the

90

dancers. This undoubtedly works in many cases but not always, for some ballet dancers have a habit of subtly anticipating the beat of the music that can be quite confusing to a guileless conductor. In such a case the best policy is to adhere firmly to what you believe to be the correct tempo, and then hope for the best.

My favorite story illustrating this is the one told to me by the late Emil Cooper, who had probably conducted more ballets in his life than most other batonists. Once he conducted a solo for a famous Russian ballerina. They had worked together for some time, but during orchestra rehearsal, things went from bad to worse. Finally the ballerina interrupted.

"Emil," she cried exasperatedly, "we are not together. Please watch my feet!!!"

"I *am* watching your feet, my dear," said Cooper calmly, "and that is probably why we are not together."

Summing up, it can be said that the technical skill required from an opera conductor goes far beyond what is ordinarily demanded in symphonic conducting. I believe it was Fausto Cleva who said that a well qualified opera conductor should do at least a competent job of leading a symphony, but that the reverse was by no means true. This statement was borne out by the experience of a prominent European maestro, a past master in the conducting of very difficult contemporary symphonic works, who was scheduled to make his debut in opera, conducting a technically not very difficult work. He had to cancel at the last moment, because of "illness." (Only the insiders knew that the "illness" was in reality the maestro's inability to keep chorus and orchestra together!)

This again leads back to the old suggestion that the opera conductor most likely to succeed is the one who has served his apprenticeship in years of coaching, chorus directing and backstage work in a professional opera theatre. Unluckily, few American conductors have this opportunity. And yet, due to local conditions and pressures, a conductor may have to take over the assignment of leading an opera for which he is poorly prepared. He cannot become a master overnight, but he can at least approach the task with humility, study a great deal in its preparation, and try to learn as much as possible during the process of rehearsing the work. And he should never forget that in spite of all his skill on the symphony podium, he is not much more than a beginner in this difficult and unfamiliar medium.

All that has been discussed up to this point concerns only the technical skills required in opera conducting. Even though some of them may sound frightening to the novice, their complete mastery is not enough to insure the valid and exciting rendition of a work of the musical theatre. It is a pity that many opera conductors feel — if they do not actually say so — that their task is merely to coordinate, to "keep things together." The result of this attitude is likely to be an efficient kind of boredom. No matter how excellent the singers may be, no matter how imaginative the visual aspects of the production, the real inspiration in an opera performance comes from the podium. Even though critics will sometimes succinctly state that "Maestro X conducted *the orchestra*" when they review an opera production, the effect that an inspired conductor has on each and every member of the cast defies description. The best illustration of this was given to me when I once asked a leading tenor of the Metropolitan Opera whom I had heard in two different operas within the same week why in performance A his singing had struck me as merely competent, while in performance B it was superbly artistic. "Because," he said, "conductor A only saw to it that I kept together with the orchestra, but conductor B is a genius: he inspired me with the true meaning of the music!" Perhaps it is discouraging to tell this story to fledgling conductors, or even to those on the ascendancy, since no amount of study can make a genius out of a mediocrity, and not every conductor of opera can or should be a genius. But the one who is not, who possesses little more than average talent, still incurs the responsibility of searching in his task far beyond mere technical competence. Most of all, he must realize that the soul of the opera is on the stage, that the conductor therefore functions not just as a musical coordinator but as a "stage director of sound." He must gear every musical detail to the exact pace and expression of the action. He must also try to understand the dramatic justification of every part of the music, vocal or orchestral. It is outright stodgy for an opera conductor to say, "the composer writes andante, so I am taking it andante." There are a hundred ways of taking an andante, and the only right way is the one that is prompted by the happenings on stage or by the psychological processes behind these happenings. In opera, it is far better to use some alterations of the tempo not indicated by the composer but demanded by the action than to follow literally every written instruction and lose the dramatic intensity! And if there is any first commandment in opera, it is the rule that every sentence must be taken at such a speed that the words can be understood. Opera always rests on words, never just on singing!

In this connection a thought might be given to the practice, very common in the United States, of presenting operas written in Italian, German or French in their original languages. This not only makes it impossible for the audience to follow the words, but it also frequently forces the singer to convey a verbal message in a language which he himself does not speak or understand. This may be aggravated by the fact that he may not even have studied the meaning of his words in great detail, leaving him with a rather sketchy idea of the thoughts he is to project in his singing. I am not attempting here to pass judgment on the practice of performing in a foreign language — a rather hackneyed controversy and limitless in its scope. My concern in simply with how conductor and singers can meet such an unusual challenge.

Unfortunately our audiences quite often have the tendency to discount the dramatic contents of an opera and to treat its performance as if it were a concert in costume. This attitude is, of course, even more prevalent when the work is performed in a foreign tongue. As conscientious performers we cannot counteract it vigorously enough. Opera is either a dramatic art or no art at all, and if the spectator uses the fact that he cannot understand the words as an excuse for the neglect of dramatic values, then he should be reminded that it was he who demanded the foreign language in the first place! If the work is to be performed with artistic integrity, the only road open to the performers is to treat the words as if they were in English: to give them the same intensity and projection as if everyone could understand them, and not to use them as a mere basis for vocalizing! The conductor and stage director must play a very important part in this process. They both must urge the singers to be fully aware of the dramatic content of the work, to study every nuance of its literal meaning, and to pronounce the words with the greatest intensity that they are capable of. The reward of such a rigorously enforced policy may be that in performance the language barrier will seem to disappear at least temporarily, and the listeners will react to the words almost as if they could understand them.

Since opera is not the only form of the musical theatre presented in our society, it is quite natural to ask what requirement a conductor must meet in an operetta, a musical, or a play with music. Technically there is not too much difference. The problem of distance and its effect on synchronization, the need for flexibility and the ability to improvise, and the difficulty in creating a correct balance between stage and pit are all encountered to some extent in every one of these categories.* Only the artistic responsibility amounts to less, since the musical substance of these art forms tends to be more lightweight and less symphonically formal. However, one additional skill is needed: the ability to follow a spoken dialogue on stage with a flexible musical accompaniment.

What makes the conducting of opera different in a practical sense from that of any of the mentioned forms is the social position of the conductor. In opera he is at the very pinnacle of the operation and only answerable to the composer. (Since the composer is often dead, this may be a stretchable responsibility!) If the stage director, the choreographer or one of the leading singers would like him to change a tempo for instance, they must present this in the form of a polite request, preferably in private. Not so in a musical or operetta. There any number of people, from the producer down to a secondary comedian, have a right to demand changes from him, to order them, so to speak. And since in a musical the printed score is not the holy book we are accustomed to treat it as in opera, he has no basis to defend himself. If the leading lady feels that she is not heard well enough in a song, she will tell him to "cut out the brass"; if the choreographer wishes to add another dance number, he will call for a repeat of the last chorus of the duet; if the lighting director needs more time for a light change, he will instruct him to repeat the interlude, and so forth. Small wonder that the conductors of musicals are paid more money than those of operas!

---

* The balance in this type of production can sometimes be improved by the use of microphones for the singers, a practice which is, of course, strictly taboo in opera!

There are now indications that the number of opera productions in this country will be rapidly increasing during the next few years. For that reason it is important that a generation of conductors be trained who realize that opera conducting is not a spare time occupation and who will be able to maintain dignified technical and musical standards. We may never have the array of small and middle-sized theatres that Germany has and that provide such a natural training ground for all kinds of opera personnel. Yet by calling attention to the problem consistently and by creating more and more opportunities in workshops and civic companies, we may at least succeed in establishing levels of competence among our opera conductors that will be equal to those generally found among the leaders of our symphony orchestras.

Chapter 8:

High Priests or Salesmen?

A brief discussion on soloists.

When Franz Liszt once referred to another famous virtuoso as an "agent voyageur en musique" (a traveling salesman of music), he was undoubtedly exaggerating on purpose and perhaps not entirely without malice. It is true that the idea of a highly-acclaimed instrumentalist playing the same two or three concerti in twenty cities across the continent, all within four weeks time, must evoke at least a surface vision of commercialism. But how meaningful is this vision? Can a man really reach the human heart with his music when he is only bent on "selling his wares"?

Let us take a closer look at these "agents voyageurs." How do they feel about their assignments, and what is their position in relation to the orchestra?

Ask any American symphony manager. He will tell you that the soloists, vocal or instrumental, are the lifeblood of his organization. No matter how fine the orchestra may be, no matter how inspiring its conductor, it is the choice of soloists that makes the difference at the box office. Suppose the orchestra of a small or medium-sized city wishes to announce its season. Will the announcement read:

THE CIVIC SYMPHONY OF GREEN GULCH, WEST DAKOTA
 Bartholomew H. Cavalieri, music director and conductor,
 will present six subscription concerts, featuring Beethoven's
 Seventh symphony, Berlioz' Fantastic symphony, Tchaikovsky's
 Fifth, etc., with the assistance of some prominent soloists . . .

I hardly think so. But perhaps it might read:

THE CIVIC SYMPHONY OF GREEN GULCH, WEST DAKOTA
 Bartholomew H. Cavalieri, music director and conductor,
 will present six subscription concerts, featuring as soloists:

BIRGIT NILSSON (soprano), ISAAC STERN (violin), VAN CLIBURN (piano), and LEONARD ROSE (violoncello) and presenting some outstanding works of the classical and contemporary symphonic literature . . .

This second way is much better. Why? Is it all a matter of hero-worship?

Generally speaking, people in the small towns of the United States are regionalists. They are very proud of their regional and local institutions, and they will tell you with great fervor why they think that life in their hometown is far better than in the big city, in any big city. "The big city is nice for a short visit, but I wouldn't want to live there," we are told.

In music, things are different. There nothing is considered good enough unless it bears the seal of approval of the national capital, New York in this case. Famous artists appear in very small towns and are being paid exorbitant fees. Their internationally known names exude a glamor that cannot be procured in any other way, and for this people are willing to pay a high price. The sleepy little town in the South or Southwest can proudly raise its head when it is able to present a soprano who has appeared at La Scala a week earlier. Time and again we find that a very fine local artist has a much harder time filling the auditorium than a third-rate one who is sent from New York. Quality alone is not enough: only the enthusiastic advance publicity from the big city makes people happy! It probably started during the last century when Jenny Lind toured the country and appeared in a vast number of small towns. These towns are still dreaming of her. Only now there are a hundred Jenny Linds, and although none of them are cheap, the price varies considerably from the most to the least glamorous.

This is why our symphony orchestra in Green Gulch must have well known soloists in order to survive. Of course, many of the people in town would like it better if the entire series were played by the New York Philharmonic under Leonard Bernstein. But this they cannot afford; nor does the New York Philharmonic have the time to appear live in all the Green Gulches of the nation. So one relies on the guest soloists for true audience excitement, and for the conductor it is the better part of wisdom to familiarize himself with this phenomenon and to face up to all the problems that it may create for him and his orchestra.

Practically every symphony orchestra in the United States hires nationally known guest soloists. Therefore, a handful of singers and instrumentalists on the rosters of a dozen managements in New York and two or three other cities must satisfy the needs of several hundred orchestras. In order to do this they must work quite hard, and the more famous they are, the harder they work. No one can say that the life of rushing from hotel to taxi to plane and to another hotel, another plane, sleeping in unfamiliar beds every night, eating unfamiliar and often not very good food, meeting hordes of people at noisy parties, and in between delivering performances that should never be less than perfect, is an easy life. The sheer physical feat of a violinist playing the Mendelssohn Concerto on Monday night, the Brahms on Wednesday, a solo recital on Thursday, and the Beethoven on Saturday, each in a different city, with different orchestras, and with long trips in between, commands the utmost respect. But if the artist, in addition to this, possesses the ability to present an inspiring performance each time, then he is almost superhuman. This is what our audiences recognize and what they will gladly pay for.

Playing or singing recitals is far from easy: nothing is easy that puts you in the limelight for two hours during which your concentration must never slacken. But at least a recital is repeated any number of times with few changes and therefore with a minimum number of hazards. Not so an orchestral solo appearance, where the soloist depends on orchestra and conductor to such an extent that an inferior performance on their part may seriously detract from his own accomplishment. Being drowned out by an overly loud orchestra is one of the lesser evils. It is much worse when a conductor, through lack of instinct, fails to gauge accurately the speed of a highly technical passage and thereby forces the soloist into a labored and strained rendition. What was to be a breathtaking display of virtuosity thus turns into the uneasy negotiating of an obstacle course with little joy communicated to the audience.

Small wonder then that the life of a traveling solo artist is not free from apprehension. To the layman it may all look like a combination of glamor, a luxurious life, high fees, continuous excitement and the general inebriation of success. But what does the famous violinist really think as his plane slowly descends for a landing at Green Gulch airport? "I have never played in this town before. What kind of an orchestra do they have here? This man Cavalieri, what is he like? Does he know his job? Has he conducted the Tchaikovsky concerto before? Will he know what to do about the triplets in the first movement so that I won't have to watch him instead of his watching me? What are their woodwinds like? Will the pitch of the clarinet in the second movement throw me off balance? And what about the big accelerando in the third? Will it feel like a ton of bricks? Who picked the Tchaikovsky anyway? I wish I were playing the Bruch — less risky. Well, you never know in this business . . ."

There is no denying that the work of a guest soloist with an orchestra can give rise to all kinds of crises, particularly when the soloist is a person of out-standing professional reputation but orchestra and conductor are no more than competent, if that! Minutes earlier, conductor and orchestra only knew the soloist from his recordings, and he did not know them at all. And now suddenly they are in rehearsal, being involved in the responsible and intimate activity of trying to make beautiful music together. A few minutes will surely be needed to "feel each other out," to get each other's bearings. After that it will soon be obvious what this event is to be: a happy meeting of minds and souls, a blissful sharing of joys through the medium of music, inspiring enough for all concerned to overlook small imperfections — or a lucrative but utterly thankless job for the soloist and a nightmare of fearful drudgery, of openly evidenced inadequacy for the musicians in the orchestra and, of course, for their conductor.

96

When I speak of "a nightmare of fearful drudgery," I do not mean to imply that this is what a conductor should regularly expect from the work with a guest soloist. It is only one of several possibilities and, fortunately, not a very likely one. Most guest soloists are very gracious people who will show it enthusiastically when they are pleased with the conductor and orchestra and who will cover up to the best of their abilities when they are not. The average soloist is a realist. He knows that he cannot expect the same qualities from a provincial orchestra as from the New York Philharmonic or the Boston Symphony. He knew that when he signed his contract. But he also knows that his fee for the concert is bigger than that of any other participant, including the conductor. In fact, if it is what is considered a big fee, it may be as much as the combined pay of orchestra and conductor! Considering this, it is not hard to be gracious even when things go wrong here and there. Certainly a soloist who grimaces each time a horn player cracks on a high note or sneers each time the intonation in the strings is less than perfect will not make many friends.

My own experiences with guest soloists have been uniformly positive — in fact, so much so that I even wonder whether they are in any way typical of the general situation. I remember perhaps two instances when a soloist would show a certain aloofness in his attitude. But this never lasted longer than the first ten minutes of the rehearsal. All the soloists that I have had the privilege to work with were as a very minimum polite and gracious. The majority of them were outgoing, warm-hearted human beings who seemed to enjoy every moment of their work. Needless to say, such an attitude cannot help but be reciprocated by orchestra and conductor.

On the other hand, it is for the conductor to realize what is necessary to make the relationship with the soloist a happy one. He must, of course, not act as if the work with the soloist were an assignment of secondary importance, an unpleasant distraction in the process of rehearsing Brahms' First Symphony that should take as little time as possible. However, even though he ought to give the solo number (or numbers) his undivided attention and the best he has to offer, he also should realize that it is the soloist's show. He cannot try to dominate the soloist, not even in a work as symphonic as Brahms' Second Piano Concerto. He should take the musical and interpretative impulses from the soloist but then treat them as if they had sprung from his own mind and heart.

Never try to argue with a soloist about tempi, phrasing or any other aspect of the interpretation! I once witnessed a scene where a conductor (not a very famous one at that!) insisted that the violinist start a retard in a classical concerto two bars earlier than he had planned. The violinist gave in, after a brief struggle, but he resented it bitterly. This seemingly trifling episode marred the relationship between the two artists, and as a result their collaboration was none too successful. Perhaps the conductor ought to bear in mind in his work with a soloist (and I am for the moment referring to instrumental soloists only; singers are a separate problem): he (the conductor) is of course expected to know a concerto very well before he starts to rehearse it. He has undoubtedly studied the score for many hours, heard it many times, perhaps listened to recordings of the work, perhaps even played the solo part himself at one time or another. However, his knowledge of the work, no matter how thorough, must appear superficial by comparison with that of the soloist, who has spent untold hours with the instrument preparing his part and who may have played it in public fifty times before. When the rehearsal begins, the soloist — even if he is not of the very first rank — has in his mind an exact disposition of where every note belongs. This disposition may have been arrived at by purely musical reasoning, or it may be prompted by the need to cover up certain technical problems. Be this as it may, any attempt to upset it at this stage would be foolish. It would be the same as telling an architect, after he had spent weeks drawing the most detailed plans of a dwelling, that he should move the living room from the north to the south side of the building!

A few years ago an occurrence of this kind received a great deal of publicity. The protagonists were a world famous pianist, a world famous conductor and a first rate orchestra. Soloist and conductor disagreed over the tempi in Brahms' B♭ Major Piano Concerto. After all attempts to compromise had failed, the conductor finally announced to the audience that he was taking the tempi requested by the soloist, although he did not agree with them. Such a procedure may have seemed extreme to some, and yet it was extremely honest. It accentuated the fact that the pianist was given the freedom to choose his own tempi. At the same time it protected the conductor who, in the case of a work that requires such intense orchestral involvement, may not have been at his best, taking tempi that he could not feel.

Not all differences of opinion between soloist and conductor are as serious as this one, and so in most cases a settlement is reached and the soloist's tempi are taken (without any announcement to the audience!). This is as it should be. Sometimes however a conductor feels that he must assert himself, and the results may be deplorable. Beethoven's Violin Concerto is a work that almost invites such a clash of personalities. Everyone of us has heard at least one performance of the work in which the conductor would start the orchestral introduction of the first movement at a carefree ♩ = 116, whereupon the violinist would play his own main theme at an emotion-laden ♩ = 96! This can no longer be excused as a "modification!" Or perhaps it was a last movement, in which the soloist would play the opening theme with all the sensuous beauty of his G string at an extremely deliberate ♩. = 72 while the conductor, in the ritornello of the orchestra, would "pick up" the tempo with a country-dance animation of ♩. = 88! I suppose that within the framework of Beethoven's thematic material both speeds could be justified, but certainly not in the same performance! Perhaps this will take some self-denial on the conductor's part, but would it not be better to be generous and help the instrumentalist, rather than carry a quarrel before the audience? There have been occasions — one of them fairly recently — when a soloist would walk out on a conductor because he could not make him see the tempo his way. This should not be necessary. There is no need to change

98

the Concerto for Violin and Orchestra into a Concerto for Orchestra and Violin. When in most cases of a difference of opinion on a tempo the soloist's will prevails, this is not only because it is natural and because all textbooks tell you that this is the way it should be done. It may also be for a subtle psychological reason: by far the most common situation of playing a concerto in the United States is one in which the soloist is an artist of national or international reputation, whereas conductor and orchestra enjoy no more than small town respectability. Quite naturally a certain humility is felt toward the "name artist," and his wish automatically becomes law, not only in the choice of the tempi, but also in such external matters as stage lighting or the way the bows at the conclusion of the piece are to be taken. But what happens when the relationship is reversed? I once attended a rehearsal of one of this country's major symphony orchestras, the conductor being one of the top half dozen in the field. The soloist was an already well known but still very young pianist who obviously was in awe of the great conductor. In the beginning of the third movement of the concerto, the maestro's tempo was obviously too slow for the soloist. A stop was made.

"Could we take it just a little bit faster?," the pianist pleaded.

"Of course, my boy," came the smiling answer from the maestro. The movement was started again — at exactly the same speed as before. No further comment was made by the pianist.

Since it is customary in this country to hire first-rate soloists for appearances with orchestras and conductors that may be artistically far inferior to them, a certain amount of friction is always within the realm of possibility. However, much of this can be avoided if both soloist and conductor will follow a few simple rules:

1. The conductor should never start a rehearsal with the soloist or soloists without introducing the guest performer, or performers, to the orchestra. By this simple device a direct human relationship between all participants is immediately established. After that, members of the orchestra are likely to be alert and generally on their best behavior when otherwise they might just be "doing a job." On the other hand, the soloist, who probably will be received with applause when the introduction is made, will also be more relaxed and feel among friends.

2. The soloist should be gracious when he meets the members of the orchestra and not save all his (or her) smiles for the audience. No matter how famous he is, he should never act with the orchestra as if he were Gulliver among the Lilliputians. If he will at least show a friendly smile when introduced, or better still break the ice with a pleasant or witty remark, the musicians will be deeply grateful and do their best in order to please him.

3. Soloist and conductor who work together for the first time or who have never performed the programmed work together should not start the orchestra rehearsal without a preliminary communication concerning the interpretation of the work. I have often found it helpful to have a run through before the orchestra

99

rehearsal in which I would play the orchestra part on the piano. In the case of some very standard works this may seem an exaggerated precaution, but it is amazing how receptive most soloists are to it. This gives them at least a basic idea of what to expect from the conductor and thus adds to their psychological security. However, if such a procedure is considered unnecessary or impractical, at the very least there should be a brief conversation in some corner of the auditorium where a few tricky points such as tempo transitions or the extent of retards are discussed. Of course, every soloist will be flattered if the conductor receives him with the words "I have studied your recording of this concerto. Are you going to play it the same way as on the recording?" He may answer "Generally, yes. But I used to make a big retard before letter B in the slow movement. I don't do that any longer." Trifling perhaps, yes. But to my mind a far more effective way of obtaining the information than by merely asking where the retards are.

4. All participants in the operation should remember that the conductor is the mediator between soloist and orchestra and that he should never be bypassed. It does a guest virtuoso little credit if he turns to a musician and says, "First oboe, you are too loud!" Not only will the conductor justifiably resent such a lack of manners, but the oboist himself may feel that the chain of command has been violated and react poorly. The correct way is, of course, for the soloist to approach the conductor, and say in his best *con sordino*, "Maestro, don't you think the first oboe could be a little softer in this passage?" By the same token, the members of the orchestra should not address the soloist directly during rehearsal. As a possible exception from this rule it seems perfectly permissible for a violin soloist to ask the concertmaster that a certain bowing be used, or for the concertmaster to ask the visiting violinist as to his preference in a matter of bowing. However, even then it shows tact to "let the conductor in on the secret."

I think that in our day most soloists have enough sense of etiquette not to violate this rule. But I do remember a rather painful incident that I witnessed quite some time ago: It was the rehearsal for a concert in which a world-famous instrumentalist was appearing as soloist with a no more than competent conductor. From the very first moment the attitude of the virtuoso was condescending at best. Finally, during an orchestral interlude when he was apparently quite dissatisfied with what he heard, he turned around and conducted the orchestra himself with the maestro standing by helplessly! I cannot imagine anything that would have been in worse taste, and I am sure the conductor would have left the stage had his prestige permitted it.

5. A perhaps rather external but not unimportant matter: the question of bows. As soon as the soloist's number is finished, he will quite naturally shake the conductor's hand, whereupon they will bow together. The soloist may then, or upon being called back, shake the concertmaster's hand also. However, under no circumstances should he ask the orchestra to rise. This is the conductor's privilege! If the conductor asks the soloist to take the second or third bow by himself — which any well-mannered conductor will do — then the soloist should

realize that this bow is strictly a solo bow, and he should refrain from acknowledging the orchestra at that particular time.

It may be interesting to investigate the conductor's psychological relationship with various types of soloists. For that purpose I should like to divide the soloists into three basic categories:

1. Vocalists (singers, and sometimes narrators).

2. Instrumentalists of the "orthodox" kind: (piano, violin, perhaps viola, and cello).

3. Instrumentalists of the "unorthodox" kind — this could be anything from a double bass to a marimba.

The popularity of solo singers with audiences, especially in small or medium-sized towns, is practically boundless. This is even more true when they are comely females. When, in a small town, the financial contribution to the orchestra donated by an elderly businessman is in danger of being frozen, there is no better way to thaw it than to hire a voluptuous looking young soprano or mezzo as a soloist and to have her sing a few arias from standard operas. If this is not possible, then a tenor or even a handsome bass will do fine. In that case the contribution will be activated by way of the elderly businessman's wife.

If the singing of operatic arias is a delight to the average person in the audience, it can often spell unmitigated boredom for the conductor. Being an ambitious member of his profession, he will look for a challenge in the music that he conducts — and there is very little challenge in "Mi chiamano Mimi" or "Salut demeure." This is even less so if he happens to be a man of operatic background who need not be told where the unwritten fermatas and retards are. He may still be enthralled by the sound of an unusually beautiful voice — but for how long? Essentially the assignment is one of following the singer with accuracy, giving support without letting the orchestra play too loud, and seeing to it that things run smoothly. Some of the less "standard" selections from opera may prove to be far more interesting. One of my greatest experiences with a soloist has been the conducting of excerpts from *Boris Godounov*. The basso was Ivan Petroff, who managed to turn every word and every sound into an intensely dramatic event, to the extent that he overwhelmed an American audience while singing in Russian! Certain selections from Wagner (Liebestod, Immolation Scene) or the final scene from *Salome* would belong to the same category. This is truly symphonic material, and the singer selecting it obviously does it for more reasons than just that of vocal display. But perhaps the most sophisticated collaboration with singers would take place in such works as Mahler's *Kindertotenlieder*, Strauss' *Four Last Songs*, and Ravel's *Shéhérazade*. These works require mature artistry from both singer and conductor, and on these terms there can be no boredom.

The soloists of the second category, "orthodox" instruments, such as piano, violin, viola and cello, represent by far the greatest number and probably also the greatest challenge to the conductor. Even among these soloists many different types can be distinguished: from a Serkin or an Arrau playing Beethoven to the fantastically gifted young violinist whose Paganini Concerto will bring the house down but whose Brahms may yet sound undistinguished, plus a great many between these two extremes who are neither high priests nor particularly efficient salesmen but who do a competent job for a reasonable fee. The novice conductor will soon discover that to accompany anyone of these artists is a task that requires all his available skill and attention, especially when they are the ones "in between!" Most of all he must have learned to listen with the utmost care, for even a relatively uncomplicated instrumental concerto poses problems of following that never occur in vocal literature. Even the fastest fioriture from the "Bell Song" from *Lakmé* are very plain by comparison with some of the runs in Liszt's Piano Concerto in B♭ or Tchaikovsky's Violin Concerto! Here things happen at a speed where even the highly seasoned musician is no longer able to hear every note separately. Therefore it is often necessary to resort to a "sixth sense," to develop an instinct that can anticipate what the soloist will do in the next measure. This is a special knack which not all the great conductors possess. And some possess it who are otherwise not so very great. They are then known as "outstanding accompanists."

Often an inexperienced conductor will spend many sleepless nights in frightened anticipation of his concert with a "big name" instrumentalist. "This man is so great and wonderful," he thinks. "He has played with all the famous conductors in the world. How can I possibly satisfy him with my lack of conducting experience and my third-rate orchestra? His technique is so unbelievable. How will I be able to follow him precisely on all those fast runs?" The terror is, of course, understandable. Yet a few years of accompanying soloists have taught me that this apprehension is misplaced. Artists of the first rank are usually fairly easy to accompany. They know exactly what they want, and their technical control makes every detail appear in complete clarity. It is the lesser ones that cause the problems, the ones that would like to produce certain effects but are not quite capable of doing so. The result can be a modicum of indecision and perhaps even confusion.

The clarity with which a musician of the first rank renders every one of his phrases is not the only reason why it is comparatively easy to accompany him. His superior control gives him much greater freedom and flexibility. He will of course demand the utmost from conductor and orchestra, but he will also give his own utmost in order to make this possible. And should he ever make a mistake, he will be the first one to admit it. The artist of lesser accomplishment may be so full of concern over his own technique that he transmits his fears to his collaborators. And what is worse, but fortunately does not occur too often, he may accuse them of failing him when really he himself was at fault.

An artist who is in complete control will always realize that there are places in classical concertos — I am thinking as an example of the recapitulation in the last movement of Mendelssohn's Violin Concerto where a calm, singing theme in the orchestra, played at a steady speed, is paraphrased and "engulfed," as it were, by highly technical passage work in the solo instrument — places where it is necessary for the soloist to follow the conductor. This he will do without hesitation. The lesser instrumentalist, thinking mainly of survival and due to his not quite dependable technique, will insist that *he* be followed. Should his rhythm be on the erratic side, this may be not only almost impossible to accomplish, but it will also result in a nervous and unrelaxed rendering of the orchestral theme.

The third category of solo artists — those of the "unorthodox" instruments — may include some traveling virtuosi, such as harpists, xylophonists, and even accordionists. They may be perfectly wonderful musicians (a matter of record in the case of some of the harpists), but their audience appeal is mostly due to the exotic nature of their instruments. Also, their literature is necessarily limited. An appearance of such an artist may be an enjoyable and even thrilling experience for conductor and audience, but it probably should not occur too frequently, so that the exotic character of the presentation will not wear off. Beyond that, this category also includes tangentially our more ambitious first desk men in the orchestra. To give them solo opportunities is a wise move on the part of the conductor. In orchestral music they play many solo passages of extreme responsibility. Yet all this is done for no extra money and little extra credit. Their appearance as soloists with the orchestra is a good way to reward them for their patience on both counts. Furthermore, the audience always enjoys a well played concerto on the flute, the oboe or the French horn, to name only a few, and there is enough good literature for each instrument to make the experience artistically worth while. Of course there is no reason why this same opportunity should not also be given to the leading string players in the orchestra.

When a highly competent local player appears as soloist with the orchestra, this may require a certain adjustment in the conductor's psychological attitude. The local player may not be as secure and positive as the traveling virtuoso, but he will be more flexible and accessible to suggestions. He must not only be accompanied well, but often guided at the same time. But what is most important: a musician who does not often appear as soloist with an orchestra will need relatively more rehearsal than a seasoned solo performer. In such a case the conductor should not get impatient. Certain difficult spots must be tried out repeatedly. The resulting security will benefit not only the solo performer but also conductor and orchestra.

To return to our "agents voyageurs": no matter what the relative artistic standing of soloist and conductor may be, the first condition for a successful collaboration between them is mutual respect. Never should one prejudge the other. A high fee paid to a traveling soloist is no guarantee that the recipient must be a first-rate musician. And the fact that an orchestra is poorly subsidized does not allow the conclusion that the conductor must be of limited musical ability. Musicians from very different "walks of life," professionally speaking, have gotten together to make very good music. This should be the first concern in any such situation, no matter what the accompanying circumstances may be.

If mutual respect is the first condition for a successful collaboration between soloist and conductor, then a oneness of feelings and intentions is its crowning glory. No really heartwarming performance can result unless both musicians work in the same direction and strive for the same type of interpretation. Although the conductor must be considerate at all times and never try to overshadow the soloist, he should also give to his performance all the intensity that he would give to a symphony. The orchestral part of a great concerto is far too meaningful to be treated merely with cold competence. If the soloist has a valid musical and intellectual concept of the work, which most of them do, then the conductor should use every effort to make this concept his own and to project it to the orchestra. This is what makes for a real meeting of minds, and on this level the conditions for a fine performance can be said to exist. In such a case the collaboration between local conductor and visiting soloist can become a truly stimulating experience, and the only regrets will be felt when the concert is over and the famous guest heads back to the airport.

Perhaps some traveling virtuosi and singers do receive rather exorbitant fees. Yet when the presence of a guest artist not only gives long-lasting pleasure to the audience but also causes a rejuvenation in spirit of the entire orchestra, then there is no reason to feel that he has been paid too much for his appearance.

Chapter 9:

"Freedom" of Choice

A few thoughts on symphonic programming.

Every spring, among the blooming of the lilacs and the reawakening of the birds and butterflies, a fearful task awaits the conductor and music director of a symphony orchestra: he must plan the programs for the following season. Why fearful? Could there be anything more heartwarming than to dig among the scores of great masterworks and to choose which ones to perform? Seemingly not. But what are the realities that surround this ostensibly very blissful occupation?

Let us assume that the board members who have hired our man are generally sensible people, not the kind that make long speeches about "I don't know music, but I know what I like, etc.," and who try to dictate programming policies down to the tiniest detail. No, these people are sensible, and they do not try to dictate either policies or programs. They have assured the conductor repeatedly that they trust his sound judgment as a musician and as a "salesman of culture." "You know what our problems are," the chairman of the board said to him. "We must attract more people to our concerts, or we will be in bad shape financially. Of course, we don't want you to lower your standards. Just make it all nice and attractive!"

So, with these golden words in his ear, the music director retires to his study, ready to attack his beautiful library of orchestra scores. The field is now wide open to let his wishes and desires go rampant. Or is it?

Not quite. He takes a quick look at the letters on his desk that have accumulated during the past few weeks. First, there is that letter from Mrs. Q. H. Winterbottom, the widowed heiress of a sugar fortune (she gave $500 to the Symphony last year). It is a nice, friendly letter, and it pays the maestro some beautiful compliments about the excellent job he is doing for the people of this city, about how wonderful the orchestra sounds now, etc. But, oh, that last paragraph! "Now, that the time for making next year's programs is drawing near, I hope you will give a little thought to us older folks and to our likes and dislikes. I am sure there are some people who like that modernistic stuff that you played last year, (Bartók: *Dance Suite*; Hindemith: *Symphony Mathis*; Copland: *El Salon Mexico*) but why so *much* of it? When there is such a wealth of *real* music to choose from! Of course, it is *your* decision, and I am not trying to influence you. But how about giving us some of those lovely gems that we have not heard in a long time, such as the *Marche Slave*, or the *Peer Gynt Suite*, or *Clair de lune*? I know you won't find it in your heart to turn down a simple request from an old lady . . ."

Then there is another letter. This one bears fifteen signatures, and it comes from the headquarters of an organization called Students For Cultural Progress. "Dear maestro," it says, "we know that you are a man of our time and sympathize with everything progressive. But why have you shown so little eagerness to express this tendency in your symphony programs? Surely you are not trying to tell us that the fifty-year-old *Dance Suite* by Bartók and the stodgy and old-fashioned *Mathis* are *your* idea of the new directions in music! What about the tastes of the culture-minded young people? Must they be made to feel that good music is only what their great-grandfathers liked? Why not some real contemporaries for a change: Nono, Boulez, Stockhausen, Cage? Yours for progress, etc. . . ."

Ugh! Suppose you ardent youngsters get together with Mrs. Winterbottom, and I shall take it from there. But wait — here is another letter that I haven't even opened. Oh, again at least a dozen signatures. "Dear Mr. Longhair, Our moms and dads keep complaining that your symphony concerts are not sold out. You want to know why? Because you play all that square junk that no one wants to listen to. Man, what a drag! Have the Monkees appear with your band, and we guarantee they'll be hanging from the rafters! You dig? The Mad, Mad Swingers."

Great — just what I have been waiting for! But what is this official looking airmail letter? Oh yes, I remember now. It comes from an important nationwide organization. "Dear maestro," it starts. *"Have you been fair to the American composer?* Truthfully, when was the last time you programmed a piece by Ives, by Barber, by Sessions, by Carter, by Piston?" (Must I really tell them?) "If you don't perform these composers, who will?" A good question. I wonder how Mrs. Winterbottom would answer it . . . But what is this exotic-looking envelope with the oriental drawings on it? Ah, from a music publisher. What does he want? "Dear Music Director, it gives us great pleasure to inform you that the performance materials of the works of two of the best known symphonic composers of Eastern Manchuria are now available at a discount rate. We know you will not wish to deprive yourself and your audiences of this unique opportunity." Here is another, also from a publisher. "The newly discovered Symphony in D Minor by Adolphe-Charles Adam has now been made available for performance in a scholarly edition. Please send us your order for this moving and significant work immediately." Here is something personal that I must have overlooked, hand-written: "Dear Maestro: Perhaps you are not aware that our beloved Dean Emeritus, Dr. Jeremiah Jones, wrote a full-length symphony some thirty years ago. It is a pleasing, tuneful work, not modernistic and technically not very difficult. I know your orchestra would enjoy playing it. We, the friends of the composer, feel that it would be a lovely gesture if you performed this work at the occasion of Dr. Jones' eightieth birthday next year, in recognition of all that this outstanding man has done for our cultural community . . ."

At this moment the conductor's beautiful wife enters the room. "Pardon me, darling. Ah, I see you are making the programs for next year. I am sure you won't forget the little request that the Smiths made the other night: the suite from *Swan Lake*. After all, the Smiths have been such wonderful friends . . ."

"Of course, of course. But I think I shall have a glass of wine now, and then go to bed. I can start making the programs tomorrow . . ."

Different conductors may disagree on how much of the preceding story is truth and how much is fiction. To assuage their doubts, let me say that it is not exactly autobiographical, but also that it is not wholly invented. There is no gainsaying that the conductor of a symphony orchestra is exposed to all kinds of pressures. And if his tendency should be to be a "nice guy," if he should wish to please everybody and comply with all the requests, he will soon realize that he has chosen the wrong profession. The making of enemies is a very natural activity for the music director of a symphonic organization, and if he is bent on survival, he must learn how to make enemies gracefully. This is not to say that he should ignore all the wishes of his "constituents," as it were. Since he is in a public position, he must in some ways please the public. But pleasing the public is not synonymous with having the audience decide what type of music should be played and what type avoided. The audience as such cannot decide, only individual members of the audience. And to be trite about it, what is one man's meat is the other man's poison. Therefore, he should carefully listen to all requests but then make up his own mind as to what it seems best to present.

Invariably the conductor must walk a tightrope. On one side there is the so-called popular taste: the clamor for familiar, easy-to-grasp music. This pleases the majority, for the person who recognizes a piece of music becomes an instant expert, which in turn flatters his vanity. Much of this can be translated into increased ticket sales. On the other side there is the conductor's educational function: he must develop the taste of the audience and also the potentialities of the orchestra. This involves the presentation of music which is not so easy to grasp and not as familiar. He should always strive to offer a sampling of the best in music, both classical and contemporary: music significant enough to preserve his own self-respect and yet not far enough away from the taste of the majority to lose their support.

All this will entail a great many compromises, and some hair-raising decisions must be made. If he bends over backwards in the direction of programs that seem interesting to his own searching mind, he may overtax the receptive faculties of the majority and thereby lose his audience. But if he bends over backwards in the direction of popular taste and keeps repeating the all-too-familiar, he will soon lose the more discriminating members of the audience and gradually the others, too, since an overplaying of even the most cherished works is bound to end in boredom. So he will find himself faced with two alternative methods of losing support, and in between, a slim and precarious possibility of keeping it. To find this possibility and to remain faithful to it is the ever-renewed problem of program making.

To begin with, a great deal depends on the number of concerts in a subscription series. Every conductor finds it comparatively easy to make a good program for one concert: here he can afford to be selfish and present three or four works that will be "down his alley" and that will make him appear in the best possible light. To make programs for a series of fifteen or twenty concerts is easy again, for in such an extended cycle there are enough opportunities to have every major composer and every significant musical style represented. The really difficult task is to plan a series of five, seven or ten concerts. In that case one obviously tries for a fairly complete representation of all the trends but often finds the available playing time not sufficient to do so. Important gaps are bound to occur, followed by the inevitable recriminations as to why this or that composer, this or that popular work was ignored.

I do not believe that a music director should go about the task of programming a series with computerized coldness. It is not just a question of representing every important composer and every significant style. The works offered must in some way relate to the conductor's personality. If a musician whose forte is impressionistic music should offer a heavily German-oriented series, with Mozart, Beethoven, Brahms, Mahler and Strauss in the lead, the result would in all likelihood be unsatisfactory since much of the music would sound dutiful rather than impassioned. If, on the other hand, a man of prevailingly German background, in order to show his catholic taste and his versatility, decided to offer a great deal of Ravel, Debussy, Respighi, Delius, Fauré, etc., it might not be any better since some of these works would probably be presented in name but not in spirit. Of course, it is rather tedious to have a conductor ride his favorite scores to death year after year — to have the subscribers ask each other during the summer: "What is it going to be this year, Tchaikovsky's Fifth or Tchaikovsky's Sixth? Strauss' *Don Juan* or Strauss' *Till Eulenspiegel*? Ravel's *Daphnis* or Ravel's *La Valse*? He should always attempt to create variety, and he should also

107

work steadily to improve his handling of scores that may initially have been foreign to him. But at the same time he should not forget that all the works he conducts are being presented through the mirror of his own personality, and that therefore it will be to the good of the series to let his strongest stylistic affinities put a stamp on it. Even a very outstanding conductor will occasionally "lay an egg" when he cannot find a spiritual bridge to the work he conducts. And no conductor can afford to offer his audience a basketful of "eggs!"

This delicate situation can become even more so in the case of contemporary works. Some conductors feel very little sympathy for contemporary music, and so they largely ignore it in their programming. Others love it with a passion and will perhaps present more of it than the audience is ready to receive. But then there is an ominous third group: musicians who have very little genuine liking for contemporary music but who feel that it is their duty to play it. So they offer a number of modern scores which they conduct in a businesslike fashion, never really getting involved. That such performances are likely to be a total loss and will make no friends for contemporary music need not be explained any further.

Now to the actual process of program making for the series. Even if all the pressure groups have been handled in a satisfactory fashion, the conductor is not likely to start the planning with a clean slate, for there is always the question of the soloists. In many cases they are, as it has been pointed out before, the chief selling attraction of the series. Furthermore, good soloists often line up their engagements quite far ahead of time, and if the organization wishes to obtain the services either of soloists in the topflight category or of somewhat less expensive ones that are "a good buy for the money" — to use management terminology — then it must act quickly and preferably have all its solo contracts signed by Christmas of the preceding year. Even at that the choice of soloists is not a completely free one: it depends on the funds that have been budgeted for the purpose and on the availability of the artists themselves. Since, in the process of negotiating, many modifications of the original plans and wishes will become necessary, the slate of soloists, as it appears in the final edition of the printed program, may be quite different from what conductor and board members had agreed earlier to try for.

Then comes the question of what each artist is to perform. Here again it is not simply a matter of choosing a concerto at random and asking the artist to play it. If a pianist has become famous for his rendition of the Rachmaninoff Third Concerto, it is unlikely that you will ask him to play the Mozart D Minor instead, even though it may fit better into your series. Besides that, the artist himself may express a wish concerning the work he is to perform, and in that case it will be wise to humor him since most musicians play best what they really like to play. Sometimes an otherwise logical choice must be turned down if the work in question had been played too recently on the series. Sometimes for other reasons: an audience that has not heard Tchaikovsky's Violin Concerto in six seasons will probably not be happy if the far less popular Vieuxtemps No. 4 is programmed. And lastly, the conductor will have to organize a certain balance between the various solo numbers in the series: when there are only five or six subscription concerts in the series, it is decidedly inadvisable to present both piano concertos by Chopin or two violin concertos by Mozart during the same year.

After the soloists have been engaged and their programs chosen, the next step, if it has not been taken care of earlier, is the decision on whether to present a choral work during the series. In that case arrangements with a chorus and with vocal soloists will have to be made. It is hard to advise a symphonic organization on how often it should present major choral works. This will depend on the availability of a good chorus and also on the taste of the audience. In a series of five to seven concerts, one choral work for the year will probably be quite sufficient. In fact, it is not at all certain that under these circumstances a choral work should be offered every year. If the choice is to offer one, it must again be coordinated with the already established program numbers: with a pianist being scheduled to play the Brahms Bb Concerto, and perhaps a violinist having chosen the Brahms Violin Concerto, it would be somewhat less than judicious to engage a chorus for a performance of the German Requiem.

Then, after all these contingencies have been settled, the music director is at last ready for the planning of the orchestral numbers. Symphonies and major symphonic poems will come first, then overtures and other relatively short numbers. There are many viewpoints according to which the selection of these numbers can be organized, and some of them will undoubtedly conflict with each other. Therefore, it seems safest to start with the most important principle, which is the musical balance of the entire series. No conductor should feel that the planning of a series should put him into a straitjacket and that his sense of originality should be stifled. Just the same, since there is an educational process involved, it is perhaps wise to establish certain basic principles and not to violate them unless absolutely necessary.

Without wishing to be pontifical about it, I am offering as an example a few principles that I have established for myself in making the programs for a five-concert series (which to all intents and purposes is the shortest series ordinarily encountered). I feel that in such a series there must be as a minimum requirement

a) a symphony by Beethoven

b) a symphony by Haydn or Mozart

c) one major symphonic work by Brahms — if not a symphony then a piano concerto, the violin concerto, the double concerto or the Haydn Variations.

d) a romantic non-German symphony or symphonic poem (Tchaikovsky, Dvořák, Smetana, Franck)

e) an orchestral work by Debussy, Ravel, Roussel, etc.

f) a symphony from the early Romantic period by Schubert, Schumann or Mendelssohn. If this is impossible, then at least an overture or concerto by one of these composers.

g) a major and established work from the twentieth century by Stravinsky, Hindemith, Bartók, Prokofieff, etc.

109

h) a local or regional premiere, perhaps a commissioned work.

This list is admittedly far from complete, but at least it is a basis to operate from. I have purposely left some ambiguities, especially in categories in which the conductor's personal taste and inclination may be the decisive factor. These categories include, for instance, Baroque music (works by Bach, Handel, Vivaldi, Corelli, Telemann, etc.), French works of the nineteenth century (Berlioz, Saint-Saëns, Fauré, Bizet), overtures and excerpts by Wagner, works by Bruckner, Mahler and Strauss, and finally works that do not seem to fit any particular category, such as Mussorgsky's *Pictures*, Kodaly's *Hary Janos*, Stravinsky's *Firebird* and others of the same type. Also, there are some works in a somewhat lighter vein that can sometimes be included to best advantage in a regular concert series: overtures and waltzes by Johann Strauss, the *Rhapsody in Blue* or the *Concerto in F* by Gershwin, or a "fun" piece like Ibert's *Divertissement*.

These are only the minimum requirements. Now the question arises as to how they can best be balanced against each other so that no style will be over-weighted. (For instance: having Brahms Fourth, Tchaikovsky's Fifth, Franck's D Minor and Saint Saëns' Symphony with Organ on the same five-concert series would not be very good programming!) In order to accomplish this, I have developed a system for myself that has proved most helpful. I use two sets of tabulations, which are as follows:

TABULATION I

German (or Austrian) works ....
French works ....
American and English works ....
Russian and other Slavic works ....
Works of other national origin ....

TABULATION II

18th Century ....
19th Century ....
20th Century ....

Now I proceed to select the individual scores. If, for instance, I choose Beethoven's Seventh, I put one mark in the German line of Tabulation I and one in the 19th century line of Tabulation II. If I select Bartók's *Concerto for Orchestra*, I put one mark in the line in Tabulation I that says "Works of other national origin," and one in the 20th century line in Tabulation II. Simultaneously, I list each work chosen in the program of the concert in which I intend to perform it. After about a dozen works have been chosen and the proper marks been put in each line, a trend will have been established. It is easy to tell by then whether the tendency is toward properly balanced programs, or whether there seems to be too much French or German music, whether there is perhaps too much emphasis on any one century, and so forth.

Of course this is not to imply that all the lines should be numerically equal.

It stands to reason that the average audience would not be very happy with a symphonic series if it had as many works from the eighteenth century as from the nineteenth, or if the number of Hungarian, Finnish and Latin-American works were equal to that of the German ones. It must be considered from the very beginning that there are certain areas, both of period and nationality, which by their very nature will require more emphasis than others. Conversely, if my listing should show seven Slavic works and only two French ones, I am safe in suspecting an imbalance which I must try to correct. However, I must always be careful about not upsetting one tabulation too much while correcting the other.

Although this procedure is helpful, it is far from foolproof. It will not work very well if all the Russian works are major symphonies, with only overtures and one symphonic poem on the German side. This is a matter of common sense, and the device is only offered for basic orientation. Also, decisions must be made as to which of the selected works should be well known standards and what others somewhat less familiar. Though it is necessary to offer a certain number of "chestnuts," this should not be overdone since the excessive popularity of a work may ultimately militate against it. For instance: it has become difficult to program Schubert's Unfinished Symphony in a regular subscription series, due to its having been played too much, while the same composer's great C Major symphony is very familiar but far from hackneyed, and while his third, fourth and fifth symphonies may be particularly ingratiating to an audience, due to their relatively offbeat quality. By the same token, Tchaikovsky's 1812 Overture has also by now gone well past the limit of tolerance of the ordinary symphony audience. But this factor should cause no undue concern. There are many other works that are also "chestnuts" — as for example Beethoven's Fifth, Brahms' First or Tchaikovsky's *Pathéthique* — but that are still gratefully accepted by audiences as the superb masterworks that they are.

In a medium-sized or small city in the United States, it is possibly a very sane principle to include one universally familiar score in each program: this will pacify the "steak-and-potato" kind of music lover! A music director who follows this routine will find that he can afford to be much freer and much less tradition-bound in the choice of the remaining works on each program.

The choice of contemporary works can be a major headache for the conductor. It goes without saying that when modern scores are played, many members of the audience will have to come to grips with an unfamiliar and perhaps somewhat repellent medium, and it may take all of the conductor's wisdom to make this encounter a peaceful one. For that reason he must be sure to present only compositions that he himself strongly believes in, for his own lack of conviction would transmit itself to the audience in no time. At the same time, a conductor who thinks he can discharge his obligation to contemporary music by performing Schoenberg's *Verklärte Nacht*, Stravinsky's *Firebird*, Prokofieff's *Classical Symphony* or Webern's *Passacaglia* will not be fooling anyone. The pretext that some contemporary composers wrote openly romantic works during their early years — despite the fact that some of these works are

111

well worth presenting — will not solve the issue but only dilute it. There is a great number of more advanced scores that these and other composers have written which will introduce the listeners to a modern idiom without needlessly shocking them. Sometimes it seems that even a mild shock is of a certain therapeutic value if it serves to present a fascinating new style to the audience, such as in Webern's *Six Orchestral Pieces*, provided that the work is not too long. In such a case the conductor may further the cause of contemporary music (and incidentally his own!) by turning to the audience before the piece is played and explaining in a few simple words the expressive principle and the compositional method of the score.

Sometimes an advanced score by a local composer will fare much better with an audience, for personal reasons, than if the same work had been written by a total stranger. This again is a bit of self-deception (though the composer will not mind it!), and it will not solve a problem that must be attacked on a broader basis.

All in all it can be said that no known type of programming will please everyone in the community. But at least we may hope that the number of dissenters and complainers will be small and that the music director, in his program building, will have satisfied his own conscience and a relatively large number of his listeners. For the rest he can only hope that even in the minds of those who are critical of him the good points will outweigh the bad ones. The strongest element in every artistic presentation is conviction, and the conductor who has it to the fullest extent will more easily convince listeners that are indifferent or that are openly opposed to his efforts. He should depend on this for both his classical and his contemporary interpretations. All the offerings, whether controversial or not, must in some way be designed to reach the audience, perhaps not in the sense of immediately causing the reaction of a wild burst of applause, but at least gradually and consistently.

In all probability there is no better guideline for any performing musician than the one given to us by Alban Berg when he said that "we should perform the classics as if they were contemporaries and the contemporaries as if they were classics . . ."

Chapter 10:

What Makes a Good or "Great" Performance?

In our keenly quality-conscious society most people make it a habit to get the best available value for their money, to spend a great deal of time "shopping around," and not to settle for potentially inferior merchandise if they can help it. They read magazines that tell them what to buy and what not to buy, and if no such information can be obtained, they will do the next best thing and choose a well known brand name. Such an attitude will occasionally work to the detriment of little advertised high quality products, but on the whole it keeps the consumer well protected.

How does this attitude affect our musical life? In the case of recordings it is simple: if the record collector is not particularly discriminating and if he suddenly decides that he wants to buy Brahms' Second Symphony, he will acquire the first recording of the work that he sees, or that the sales clerk recommends to him. Chances are that he will not suffer in the wake of such a procedure, for it is unlikely that he would be able to tell the difference between various performances of the work anyway. If he is more discriminating (but still a layman!), he may buy the recording made by his favorite conductor, although more likely he will act on the basis of the opinion expressed by his favorite critic in the record magazine.

With live orchestral concerts the procedure tends to be more involved. In the case of pairs of concerts given on successive days, the music lover may decide whether to buy tickets for Thursday night's concert after he has read the review of the same program on Wednesday night in the Thursday morning paper. Yet, if the program is only given once, he will have to make up his own mind as to whether it promises to be worth while.

But how does he react during the concert itself? What tells him whether to like it or not? Here again there are brand names to protect the customer. If the conductor is an internationally famous man and the soloist a virtuoso of the first rank, it is probable that the concert will be of outstanding quality. Probable, but by no means certain, for musicians of great fame have their failings too. Therefore, it is an interesting game for the observing musician in the audience to try to determine what the average music lover knows or senses about the performance he hears. When he comes home from a concert raving how wonderful it was, did it really touch him so deeply, or was it simply the magic of the brand name that took effect?

To begin with, it would be very unjust to put all members of the audience into the same category. In most concerts we will find a few professional musicians in the audience, representing one extreme, and a few people who are there for irrelevant reasons and whose relationship to music is nil, representing the other. In between these two poles there is the large crowd of laymen for one reason or another devoted to serious music and with a greater or lesser degree of musical erudition. They are numerically in the majority, and for that reason they are the strongest factor in the reception accorded a live musical event. Many of them may be amateur musicians, or at least may have played an instrument at one time. Others may have no direct practical experience with music, but they have heard enough to acquire a fairly reliable sense of discrimination.

How sensitive are these people as a group? Can they really tell a good performance from a bad one, and are they courageous enough to give expression to their feelings?

When you explore these issues with individual music lovers of average background and find out how limited their judgment is, then it must amaze you that an audience as a body generally does not misjudge performances too severely. Apparently there is a process of amalgamation that is responsible for it. One might compare it with the second violin section in a mediocre orchestra: there are twelve or fourteen violinists, and hardly one of them is worth listening to. Yet when they all play together, the effect is not bad at all!

Therefore, it would be quite wrong to condemn the average audience as being insensitive to the merits of a musical performance. Only, how sensitive they are will largely depend on the nature of the performance itself. Advance publicity of the performers naturally has a great deal to do with it, but it is not everything. In a positive or negative sense, there is always a certain amount of sincere and spontaneous reaction. In this country displeasure is frequently covered up by inbred good manners, but it may still be noticeable — not as noticeable, though, as enthusiasm. When a concert audience errs in its judgment, it almost invariably errs on the benevolent side: an artist who really does not have very much to offer may be warmly applauded. But it is hard to imagine that an outstandingly good performance would be received with coldness or hostility.

My own experience has been that the greatest sensitivity of an audience of laymen in music lies at the extreme ends of the scale. They can always recognize a performance that is overwhelmingly good or one that is miserably bad. The area of the greatest number of misjudgments lies in between: with performances that are neither bad enough to make one cringe nor good enough to be unforgettable. Particularly in the Classical symphonic literature many errors are made. When one conductor offers a performance of a Classical symphony that is technically clean but replete with wrong tempi and phrasing and generally uninspiring, and then another performs the same work with the right tempi and phrasing and with a great deal of vitality but technically in not quite as flawless a fashion, chances are that the first conductor will meet with a much more enthusiastic audience reception. Basically, this is understandable. Anyone can tell when the sound of the violins is scratchy or when the horns crack on high notes. But to judge whether the speed of the andante moderato was correct takes a certain amount of knowledge. Only in the case of a completely superb performance will these considerations become meaningless: here there is so much power of conviction in every note that the sensitive listener succumbs to it immediately and finds it futile to ask questions as to the correctness of details.

All in all it is quite obvious — and it seems to me that there is no harm in admitting it — that only a comparatively small amount of the music offered in a symphony concert reaches the hearts and minds of the audience; the rest is heard but not listened to. This small amount increases in the case of an outstandingly good performance where the music assumes a compelling quality that grips even the casual listener and holds him in its spell or, curiously enough, in the case of an extremely bad one whose negative effect is so striking that it even interferes with an uninvolved housewife's planning of the next day's menu. But in the normal, quite-good-but-not-outstanding performance, many minds are far away, and only an occasional fortissimo chord or the end of a movement will recall them from their dreams and remind them of the purpose of their presence. It is true that it requires some mental discipline to listen to a symphonic work without allowing the mind to wander. Perhaps it is unfair to expect this discipline from more than a small elite in the audience. But, be this as it may, the commercial that says "all meat, no bones — all food, no waste" can hardly be made to apply to the listening process of a concert audience.

If basically this is the limited connection which exists between performers and audience, what are the qualities in the performance itself that reach the listeners, that leave an imprint on the minds of the majority? There are a few clear and unmistakable factors. The first is precision. Even the not-very-sophisticated listener can tell whether a chord is attacked by all instruments at the same time or whether it appears on the sound surface in lackadaisical instalments. He can tell whether pizzicati are disciplined or ragged and whether there is a unity of spirit in the singing of a broad string melody. Some help in this is offered by the visual element: it would hardly be conducive to musical precision if a few violin bows at the back stands moved in a pattern of their own, ignoring the discipline of the majority. Furthermore, it is not only the element of precision that makes a visual impact: in a vital, animated performance you can tell by the looks of the musicians' movements that they like what they are doing, that they are doing their share not just dutifully but enthusiastically. (Only the faces of routined musicians often retain their blasé expressions, no matter how animated their playing may be!)

The next element, in order of impact on the audience, would be dynamics. A good conductor has the ability to make an orchestra play beyond ordinary loudness (which in itself is negative); that is, to fill the loudness with meaning and excitement. Attempting to translate this into more realistic terms, it means that he will assign to each instrument or group of instruments the right degree of loudness. If, for instance, in the tutti fortissimo chord of an early Beethoven symphony the trumpets should stand out as the clearly dominating sound, this would render an impression of vulgarity rather than intensity. But if the same chord is balanced in such a fashion that the string sound is dominant, with woodwinds and brasses supplying a strong backing yet without any brass instrument being allowed to stand out, then the impression will be one of satisfying vigor and nobility. By the same token a piano that is merely soft will mean very little to the listener, but a piano that is soft and singing, obviously conveying an expressive message, will attract his attention and be pleasing to him. It is also very important what a conductor is able to do with the sound of an orchestra at the outer limits of its dynamic scale, particularly in romantic music. When the musicians play an "uninstructed" pianissimo, it will usually materialize perhaps not as a mezzo forte, as Verdi pessimistically assumed, but as a cold piano, without any definite meaning. But if the conductor knows how to coax them into giving the absolutely softest sound they are capable of, still filling it with intensity, then the effect on the audience may be one of tremendous excitement. Equally exciting — in Romantic or contemporary music — is a fortissimo that

115

"takes the roof off," again with the proper elements of sound prevailing: balanced! This can only be procured if every musician makes a determined personal effort toward its attainment. The reason why one does not hear it more often is a twofold one: some conductors lack the imagination that makes them desire such a sound and are satisfied with a compromise; others may possess the imagination, but lack the persuasive power to obtain it from the orchestra.

Another important and sometimes obvious criterion in the quality of a symphonic performance is intonation. This may affect the unsophisticated listener with varying degrees of intensity. Faulty intonation is generally most easily detected in a unison of string instruments where it produces the sensation popularly referred to as "the fiddles sounding sour." This contingency may be a conductor's nightmare since, despite the best of intentions, he may be unable to control it. When the precision of a forte chord is not there, or when a pianissimo lacks intensity, it usually means that the conductor gave up before the time, that he was not exacting enough to summon the best efforts from the musicians. But when "the fiddles sound sour," he may have gone to the ends of the earth to unsour them but was helpless in the face of the technical incompetence of some of the players! Still, the bad effect will noticeably dim his own accomplishment.

The intonation of woodwinds and brasses is an altogether different matter. In this area the average musician in an American orchestra is an absolute fetishist: he may be rather overly generous in condoning his own or someone else's faults in regard to dynamics, expression, phrasing, etc., but when in his solo the B♭ was one eighth of a tone too high, he will spend a sleepless night over it. Perfectionism of any kind should of course not be laughed at. Only this kind of perfectionism is one that often goes far beyond the sensitive limits of any member of the audience, and being an obsession, it can easily work to the detriment of other, more vital factors. Despite all fetishism, the pitch in woodwinds and brasses, even in better known American orchestras, is often less than perfect. This is very annoying to the musicians, but the average listener in all likelihood is blissfully unaware of it!

The most elusive one of all the major factors that influence the quality of a symphonic performance is phrasing. Intonation, rhythm, beauty of tone and proper dynamics are all qualities that we have a right to expect from every well schooled professional instrumentalist. Correct and beautiful phrasing on the other hand is the earmark of an intelligent and mature player, and often we find very little of it in the playing of a musician who is richly endowed with all the other qualities. First desk men in a professional orchestra should always be secure and artistic in their phrasing, but with the others it is not so certain. It may take a great deal of patience and persuasion — not to speak of knowledge and artistry — on the part of the conductor to make this quality all-pervasive. A warm, expressive legato and an incisive, resilient staccato are its two main elements, but there is too much in between to attempt mentioning it here. The most difficult fact about phrasing is that it cannot entirely be deduced from the

116

printed symbols. In order to be valid it must rest upon a sound sense of style. Instrumental teachers are often either ignorant or careless in this respect: they exhaust their wisdom by either saying "play it slurred," or "play it tongued." Mezzo legato for instance is never mentioned by this type of teacher, and a conductor should therefore not be surprised if its occurence in a subsidiary part forces him to deliver a brief lecture on the subject!

Audiences, who are tolerant to many facets of intonation, are however instinctively sensitive to phrasing and instinctively disturbed by its absence. They may not know the exact reason, but when they hear a Mozart symphony that is not properly phrased, they will realize that it is not "good Mozart." For that reason it is wise for the conductor to work out his ideas on phrasing a work to the minutest detail and to make sure in his study of the score that all of it is logically and stylistically justifiable since this elusive quality may make the difference between a vital and a lethargic performance.

One final ingredient that is very essential in the playing of an orchestra, and without which a good performance is unimaginable even in the ears of the less educated listener, is the beauty of tone of individual instruments and of groups or choirs of instruments. Here also the conductor's influence is of necessity limited, particularly when his assignment with the orchestra is only temporary. The beauty of tone of a first oboe, a first clarinet or a first horn is something he cannot obtain by coaxing. Each player must have developed it through years of study, based on natural talent. It is something to be grateful for when it exists, just like the beautiful voice of a tenor or a soprano. What can be developed — within reason — is the beautiful sound of a group, particularly of the strings. But this may be a slow process, and not too much of it can be done while preparing a single concert. For the permanent conductor of an organization the development of a beautiful sound in the various choirs is a duty that he must not shy away from. And it is always pleasing to hear a listener remark on the warm string sound after a concert.

Of course, this beautiful sound of groups can only be developed if every player in the group meets certain standards. This means that the permanent conductor of an orchestra, in auditioning new members, must not only see to it that they are proficient players, but also that the playing style of each of them will blend well with the respective choir. When this quality is developed through generations, it can become the factor that will make an organization world famous. You speak of the strings of the Vienna Philharmonic, the woodwinds of the Boston Symphony, or the brasses of the Concertgebouw, symbolizing in each case the highest possible accomplishment of ensemble playing.

However, the impression should not be given that the role of a guest conductor regarding improved beauty of sound is hopeless. Far from it! In fact, sometimes improvements will take place without his actively working for them. It is not at all unusual to hear people say during the concert of a guest conductor: "It sounds like a different orchestra tonight!" The psychological reason for this is very interesting. First of all, the guest conductor is in a better position in

117

relation to the orchestra than the permanent conductor since every orchestra likes a change once in a while. Furthermore, he can afford to be generous about certain weaknesses since he does not have to live with them for any length of time. This perhaps, in the eyes of the musicians, puts him into advantageous contrast with the permanent conductor, who never ceases to apply pressure toward the improvement of every single aspect of the playing. The comparison between the permanent conductor and a guest conductor of an orchestra is approximately the same as between a woman's husband and her lover: after years of — more or less — drudgery, she is suddenly made to feel young and beautiful again! The guest conductor, anxious to keep everyone in good spirits, will probably try his best to make the musicians feel that they play very well. As a result, they actually will play better than at other times! Jean Martinon, expressing the same thought, said about guest conducting: "You use the instrument which is given to you, and you try to get the best for your own concert, but you don't mind about the deep problems. If one section happens to be a little weak, you leave it as it is."

If the guest conductor has the knack, in addition to these favorable odds, to give the musicians a feeling of relaxation and enjoyment, to be less a taskmaster and more a friend, then the results, at least as far as the beauty of sound goes, may indeed be spectacular. It would be foolish of him not to make at least a try in that direction.

All the above-mentioned elements are necessary in the making of a good performance. And a really good performance is no small accomplishment when you think of the many that are mediocre or outright bad. By definition, a good performance would be one in which the conductor and all the musicians give the best that can reasonably be expected from them.

But then there is the "great" performance, and this is an altogether different matter. There is nothing reasonable about a great performance. It is a miracle that cannot be accounted for. Perhaps its outstanding characteristic is the fact that the orchestra as a whole plays far better than the sum total of its individual players. All the participants feel a strange uplift, and as a result they produce a quality that they did not know they possessed. One has the feeling of a telepathic force taking effect between conductor and musicians, a force that makes them play music of the kind that one cannot rehearse. A musician of the Vienna Philharmonic described this phenomenon very well when he said about Furt-wängler: "When he conducts, he doesn't look at us, and we don't look at him — and yet, we never play better than under him!"

It is always the conductor who causes an orchestral performance to be great. (We shall not consider here the very rare case of a concerto where an outstanding soloist carries both conductor and orchestra along with him.) The finest orchestra in the world cannot play a great performance when it depends for inspiration on a man who is no more than routinely competent. On the other hand, a little better than average orchestra can sometimes be hypnotized into playing a great performance if the man on the podium has the power to do it! Yet even the collaboration between a great conductor and a great orchestra cannot guarantee a great performance. It can only offer the probability that it may happen. Ultimately, no one can foresee if and when the decisive spark will strike.

How can you recognize a great performance? From its overwhelming psychological impact. It does not just please or even excite you, but it puts you into a complete state of turmoil that may continue long after the sound has died down. But if you really want to be sure, you must wait about twenty years. If after that time some of its details are still clearly present in your mind and excite you as if the whole thing had happened yesterday, then you may be sure that it was a great performance . . .

The average music lover is not likely to hear more than two or three dozen great performances in his life. Even at that he is lucky! It is interesting that one rarely remembers such a performance as an integrated whole. Usually it is one or several especially poignant details that remain unforgettable after everything else has faded into the background. The earliest great performance that I can recall was one that I heard only over the radio: the "Eroica," played by the New York Philharmonic under Toscanini during their European tour. I was a child then, and most of it is blurred in my mind now. But I can still hear the two opening chords, and the recollection of their intensity even now sends shivers down my spine! Later, during my formative years, I heard a number of symphonic performances that I shall never forget. There was Beethoven's Ninth under Furtwängler, which I recall with amazing clarity. Most memorable was the haunting horn solo in D Major at the end of the first movement, the unearthly first entrance of the three-four theme in the third, and the incredible F Major triad fermata on the word "Gott" in the last! Mahler's Second under Bruno Walter: unforgettable was the Ab Major minuet, notably the section with the counterpoint in the first violins, that had none of the superficial coyness so often played into it but was pure human emotion — and the absolutely spellbinding first pianissimo entrance of the chorus in the last movement! The Verdi Requiem under Toscanini: the mysteriously restrained expressiveness of the opening and the earshattering drumbeats of the Dies irae! Berlioz' *Fantastique* under Weingartner, Tchaikovsky's Fifth under Koussevitsky and, more recently, Ravel's *Daphnis et Chloé* under Munch and Shostakovich's Fifth under Stokowski. In glancing over this somewhat arbitrary array of performances, one notices the striking fact that all but one of them were led by men well past their middle age. Perhaps this kind of inspiration is not given to the very young, at least not among conductors!

I purposely refrain from mentioning great performances whose excitement was caused by the presence of a vocal or instrumental soloist. They belong in a different category. The striking phenomenon to be discussed in these pages is the type of performance in which a group of musicians, most of them of only ordinary accomplishments, stirred on by the leadership of one man, miraculously produces a musical rendition that appears to be beyond the powers of all of them.

119

This still leaves the most difficult question to be answered: what are the specific elements in an orchestral performance that make one feel it is great? It goes without saying that the great performance must possess all the ingredients of a merely good one, but what must it have in addition? Perhaps it is not so much that there are additional elements in it — with one exception to be discussed later — but that the virtues that distinguish the merely good performance must be present to a much larger extent in the great one. In a good performance you greet the presence of such virtues with grateful satisfaction; in a great one, with overwhelmed amazement.

Take the simple matter of tonal beauty. When you hear a good performance of the Prelude to Act I of *La Traviata* with clear intonation and a warm espressivo, you will probably say, "This is beautiful!" But if you heard Toscanini conduct it, you were fully convinced that this was the most heavenly sound that had ever reached your ears! Or take the element of dynamics. Every well controlled and expressive pianissimo in the lower strings has a mysterious and haunting effect. But when Furtwängler started the Ode-to-Joy theme in Beethoven's Ninth, he created a completely unreal kind of excitement that was far beyond the realm of a merely beautiful pianissimo and that no one else has ever conjured up for me again. The beginning of the last movement in Beethoven's Fifth, when the orchestra-tutti sound is clean, rich and warm, is always a wonderful moment. But when Weingartner conducted it, there was far more to it than that: even listeners not usually given to obvious imagery had visions of an emperor entering the gates of a city in a march of triumph! All these are examples of what either tonal beauty or dynamics or a combination of both can do when they are driven to ordinarily unfamiliar extents by the vision and imagination of a top-flight conductor.

A somewhat more elusive ingredient is that of clarity. Again, we must consider this a requirement in every good performance. Every conductor worthy of the name devotes his unflagging efforts to creating a correct balance between leading and subsidiary voices. He makes sure that everything important is heard, and he tries to eliminate all thickness and obscurity in the orchestral texture — this is taken for granted. But then suddenly a performance takes place that makes one feel as if he had never known the true meaning of clarity before. This happened to me when I heard Toscanini's performance of Brahms' Fourth.

It is quite common for musicians to say that Brahms did not really know how to write for the orchestra, that much of his orchestral work is actually orchestrated piano writing. We are told that certain passages will always sound muddy simply because they are not conceived for the medium. And it is, of course, easy enough to prove this by pointing out some of the arpeggios written for the lower strings which, if played on the piano, would be a sheer pleasure, but which give very little joy to a viola or a cello player. All this is true to some extent, but no one who heard *that* performance would ever have known it! I heard people say then that for the first time the Brahms Fourth sounded like an Italian opera. Naturally, this was a ridiculous statement, for the orthodoxy of the tempi and the general style of the interpretation left nothing to be desired. What struck the listeners was that possibly for the first time they could hear all the beautiful details that Brahms wrote into his score and that are often buried in the mud of poor balance. There was lucidity from beginning to end. In so many other renditions of the work the full beauty of the various details cannot emerge properly because of the conductor's attitude that might be verbalized as follows: "What do you want from me? Brahms was not a very good orchestrator. There is nothing that *I* can do about it!"

Toscanini felt that he *could* do something about it, and he did it. Undoubtedly there must have been a great many changes of dynamic marks, and perhaps even notes, plus a few slight alterations in the orchestration. But whatever they were, they had been administered with such a masterful hand that they did not register as changes and the spirit of the work remained unharmed.

Ten years after Toscanini's death and with the help of the added perspective, his standard claim that he was doing exactly what the composer had written seems somewhat ironical, at least if one takes it literally. Applied to the spirit of a score, it was undoubtedly true in the vast majority of his interpretations. But conductors have a tendency to take the spirit for granted: they are more interested in what happens to the sforzato in the second clarinet that cannot be heard unless you "do something." And, whether he admitted it or not, in this intricate area of "doing something" Toscanini's methods were apparently superb. Whatever they were, his capability of achieving complete clarity of texture has probably never been rivaled. This is not to say that other men of major stature have not found their own ways of evoking this essential virtue. Every great performance has it and must have it. Conversely, when the conductor feels, for reasons of his own, that nothing must interfere with his unbridled passion, then the standards of clarity set in his renditions may not be the very highest!

This leaves one final element which is part and parcel of a great performance and which, as I have hinted before, may be hard to find in a lesser one: simplicity. Highly-talented musicians may be complicated in their musical thinking, but great musicians are simple! The artist not quite of the first rank will often feel that he has to add something more to his interpretation — an accent here, a retard there, just one more expressive detail — to keep the audience from getting bored! The artist of the first rank, however, is so sure of the message that he has to convey that idea of boredom never enters his mind. Thus, he can afford to be simple.

During my student days I heard several of the then most prominent cellists in quick succession. Overwhelming, fantastic, phenomenal were some of the adjectives that I felt impelled to use in each case. Then I heard Pablo Casals. He was not fantastic nor phenomenal. He simply made me feel that his way was the only way of playing the cello and that anyone trying it differently was sadly mistaken. This may be the criterion of interpretative greatness in music: the basic outline of the work has been reduced to such a simple denominator and its structure is adhered to so clearly that the details fall into place and seem completely natural.

I had heard many performances of the Tannhäuser-overture before I heard Toscanini conduct the work. At the first entrance of the trombones it is — or was — traditional to make a retard, as if to say "Watch it now — be sure not to miss it — the trombones are entering with the theme!" I had heard it played with a big retard, with a small retard, with an absolutely elephantine retard, and in many other fanciful ways. Then I heard Toscanini's performance, and he made the trombones enter without any retard at all, which is, incidentally, the way Wagner wrote it! This amazingly simple way seemed more impressive than any of the others, and it was an eye opener to me.

But now it is only fair to ask why a conductor should resort to such a device if the music sounds better without it. First of all, he may not know that it does if he has not had the courage to try it. Aside from that, there are several possible justifications. One is that he uses the retard because it is traditional. ("If so many others have done it before me, then it cannot be wrong.") Then there is another possibility, and I suspect that this one is more prevalent than one would assume: in the first rehearsal the conductor found that the trombones were a little slow in their attack, forcing him into a retard. He felt that the result was not too bad. So, rather than start an argument with the trombonists about the necessity to anticipate their first note, he let them play it in their own way. He kept the retard in and kept the trombone players smiling! The third possibility — and undoubtedly the most suspect one — is that the conductor wants the retard in order to call attention to himself: it is so dramatic! This of course is a "gimmick," and it has little to do with the interpretation of great music. It is the kind of thing that a sincere and unselfish musician would not be guilty of.

In a great symphonic performance the conductor does not call attention to himself. He knows only too well that getting the message of a masterwork across to the audience and eliciting the best efforts from the musicians takes up all his available energy. He has no time for self-glorification! The "watch-the-way-I-do-this-now" attitude may have helped many podium virtuosi of secondary stature to instantaneous success, but in the sphere of great musicianship there is no room for it. This does not mean that the great conductor is not aware of being a great conductor or that he is not enjoying it! Only in popular fiction are we led to believe that a man like Toscanini was so humble that he never thought of himself, only of serving the masters whose works he conducted. Of course he served the masters, and he served them well, but at the same time he certainly knew that he as a "servant" amounted to far more than many a colleague of his who considered himself a master! A great conductor may be humble when he faces Beethoven or Mozart, but he is rarely humble in his personal life or in his public attitude. He has gained the assurance that what he does in his musical interpretations is valid and will project through its own strength. Therefore, he need not act like a clown and solicit the acclaim of the audience by devices that are obviously showy and self-centered. He may cheerfully leave this to lesser men!

Nevertheless, there are moments when even a very great musician on the podium will not rigorously stick to the printed letter of the score and will add details of his own. But they will be details well rooted in the structure of the work, so that the composer might well have approved them if he had been asked. As a good example, I recall that Richard Strauss, in conducting Beethoven's Seventh, made a tiny caesura at the beginning of the development of the first movement before the celli and basses start their pianissimo theme in C Major. This merely has the effect of clarifying the entrance of the theme without unduly dramatizing it. I do not believe that any sensible listener, upon hearing it, would have said, "Look, what Strauss does to embellish Beethoven!" The difference between this caesura and the retard in the Tannhäuser-overture is that one is done for the benefit of the work, the other for the (dubious!) benefit of the conductor. The deciding agency in all these questions must be the conductor's good taste. It stands to reason that in outwardly highly-emotional music, such as Tchaikovsky or Liszt, a certain amount of "posing" (musically speaking!) is permissible, contrary to the best practices followed in Mozart or Beethoven. At the same time, Viennese classical composers are human too: their emotion may not be as showy, but it is just as intense, if not more so. The conductor who approaches them as a soulless purist — antiseptically, as it were — does them a marked disservice.

Greatness in the conducting profession, as in any other, is given to only a very few. These men are outstanding not only in regard to their talent, but also to their character. The many others who will never achieve greatness are still under moral obligation to strive for the highest standards, to act toward their own artistic conscience as if they expected to be great some day. The reward, if not in anything else, may be in the effort itself.

Some of us may never be able to reach the top of the mountain. Disturbing as this may be, it should not make us forget that there can be great joy even in a short climb!

PART III. THE INTERVIEWS.

Chapter 11:

Background and Motivation.

I am not sure which came first, the idea of the book or the idea of the interviews. It is a fact that for a long time I had been toying with the thought of getting the reactions of some of the best known symphonic conductors to a number of problems which all conductors must face practically every day of their lives. The decision to write this book seemed to offer an excellent excuse to turn this thought into reality, so I immediately proceeded to make the necessary contacts and arrangements.

Perhaps the idea of the questions themselves will be astonishing to some, and even some of the questioned conductors themselves could not conceal their astonishment. Why should these men be interviewed? Is it that I expected their answers to be so brilliantly superior to anything that you, or I, or the music director of the Green Gulch Symphony would be able to offer? Not necessarily, although I must admit that I received a certain number of answers that were so strikingly original and stimulating that they alone would have made the whole venture worthwhile. However, my basic motivation was of an entirely different nature. This was a project that involved ten symphony conductors of the front rank, and the benefit that I expected to derive from questioning them was not so much in the answers of the single individual as in the opportunity to compare the detailed reactions of ten representative minds. Whether this effort has paid off is something which I should like to let the reader decide.

Whatever the thoughts of the reader may be, I must selfishly admit that the venture has been of great value to me personally, and in addition, it has been most enjoyable. The quiet confrontations with ten individuals high on the ladder of success in this profession and the chance to sound them out on a number of serious professional problems has given me an insight that I never could have gained otherwise, and the part of my mind that is deeply interested in psychological inquiry has been richly rewarded. I have reached a great many conclusions, some of which unfortunately I shall not be able to communicate to my readers. However, I trust that on the basis of many indications and implications, the discerning readers will reach their own conclusions.

What I do wish to communicate is that with practically no exception the conductors approached responded in a very polite and often cordial fashion. The vast majority were obviously happy to be asked their opinions on professional problems by a professional. Of the twelve conductors that I contacted, all but two granted me the requested interview, and in one of the two remaining cases it was obviously due to legitimate scheduling difficulties that the talk did not materialize. Of course it should be said that I did not approach all these conductors as a stranger. One of them, Josef Krips, is a former teacher of mine, and six others I have known through personal or professional contact of varying degrees. Only three of them I had never met before.

126

The interviews took place at the conductors' homes, in their hotel rooms, or in dressing rooms before or after rehearsals. About halfway through the series I decided to use a tape recorder rather than my notes and my memory. However, I do believe that even in the case of the interviews that took place without the benefit of the tape recorder, the quotations are reasonably accurate — at least I have made every possible effort to make them so.

As far as the questions are concerned, I decided on them in order to provide a common denominator for the interviews. Of course, it would have been tempting in many cases to improvise questions in the course of the interview — to ask Max Rudolf how the technical patterns used by him in actual conducting related to those described in his well known book, or to ask Leonard Bernstein about his ideas on conducting for a television audience — but this would have gone beyond the scope of the project and had to be discarded. It seemed much more essential to me to obtain various reactions to a standard set of problems, and the only sensible way to do this seemed to be to face each conductor with the same prepared set of ten questions, eliciting his impromptu reactions to each. (In no case did a conductor have more than five minutes to look at the questions before giving his answers.) This impromptu quality was very essential to me. An answer to a question of this type that has been carefully prepared may be a great deal more polished and refined, but it is also almost certain to lose the feeling of spontaneity that I was looking for.

The questions themselves were arrived at by various methods. I must stress the fact that it was not my purpose to identify with any tendency or attitude expressed in these questions. In fact, some of them did not originate with me at all and were simply used because I had run into them time and again, and because I was very curious how they would be received by people who could react to them in an authoritative fashion and who had obviously also encountered them many times — who perhaps were even angered by one or the other of them! Not all of the questions were the result of "conductorial thinking"; one or two had been suggested to me by orchestra musicians and at least one by a non-professional music lover.

On the whole, these questions make no claim to go beyond the spotlighting of a few scattered areas within the field of orchestral conducting. Anything more than that would have taken more time and patience than any of my illustrious subjects could possibly have given me. Even so I feel that many of the statements are extremely revealing, and well worth the average conductor's or musician's attention.

Naturally, the amount of space available did not permit me to use every answer to every question. For this I apologize profusely to any one of my famous colleagues who may feel that he should have been quoted more extensively. I had to use my own judgment in the matter of quoting verbatim from the interviews, and wherever I had to omit a possible highly pertinent opinion, I tried at least to include each conductor's reaction as part of the poll and in this fashion leave no doubt as to the position of the majority on each question.

On the other hand, I have included a number of significant statements from the interviews in the earlier chapters of this book. This had not been my original intention, but it suggested itself while writing the other chapters. In some cases it became necessary because some of the interviewed conductors had strayed away from the subject of the questions during the interviews, and several of their statements, although not directly related to what they had been asked by me, were far too good to be ignored.

Whenever I quote a statement which to me seems particularly meaningful, I have identified its originator by name. If in any case this has not been done, the reason is that I considered the opinion expressed of greater import in its collective context than as an individual statement.

The conductors interviewed were (in alphabetical order): Sir John Barbirolli, formerly music director of the Houston Symphony, now guest conductor of the same organization; Leonard Bernstein, music director of the New York Philharmonic; Sixten Ehrling, music director of the Detroit Symphony; Joseph Krips, music director of the San Francisco Symphony; Erich Leinsdorf, music director of the Boston Symphony; Jean Martinon, music director of the Chicago Symphony; Max Rudolf, music director of the Cincinnati Symphony; Izler Solomon, music director of the Indianapolis Symphony; William Steinberg, music director of the Pittsburgh Symphony; Werner Torkanowsky, music director of the New Orleans Philharmonic.*

---

* In these days the game of "musical chairs" among leading conductors is such a lively one that at the time when these lines appear in print some of the identifications given above may no longer be correct.

Chapter 12

The Ten Questions.

1. It has been stated, particularly by orchestra members, that in American orchestras the musicians often have the tendency to treat the conductor as their natural enemy. Do you believe this to be true, and if so, what are your methods of dealing with this problem?

Predictably, seven out of ten conductors brand this assumption as untrue. Two others (Krips, Martinon) unhappily declare that it is true ("and most unfair!" says Martinon), and one (Solomon) thinks that it depends on the circumstances. Rudolf and Steinberg, both saying "untrue," qualify their statements by admitting that it may be true in Europe, but not in the United States. Steinberg explains further: "In thinking of first rate orchestras in the United States, since the players are superior players, it is assumed that they are also superior human beings and therefore not susceptible to these tendencies. And," he adds, "you also have to think of American musicians as being American in their psychological makeup, which means that they are primarily doing a job." He also thinks that "their being better human beings has to do with the fact that they are paid better."

Leinsdorf, who emphatically declares that the "enemy" idea is all wrong, points out that the musicians simply "know very well when they play under their own form, and they resent it. The conductor who makes them play badly automatically becomes their enemy, but this has nothing to do with *natural* enmity!" He further explains that "the most disliked of conductors, if they know their business, are never referred to as *enemies* by the musicians." (They have spicier names for them, closer to the vernacular.)

Sir John Barbirolli claims that "orchestras want to play well, and if they sense that the conductor knows how to get good music from them, they will not treat him as an enemy. The orchestra is like a thoroughbred race horse," he says, "it senses the touch of a good rider." Ehrling finds that musicians in this country are "very cooperative and easier to work with than some in other parts of the world." Max Rudolf agrees with this, saying that "in this country musicians will do the job for the conductor as long as he does not actually insult them," and points out further that "American musicians are very sensitive to invective: certain European conductors who have resorted to invective and perhaps hurt the sensitivities of the musicians have thus become their enemies." Leonard Bernstein believes that the enemy idea is "not even a valid supposition," but explains that he never had that trouble since he started his conducting career with an orchestra whose assistant conductor he had been before. Therefore, the musicians were his friends to begin with.

Josef Krips, representing the opposite viewpoint, thinks that the enemy idea is quite valid. "Being an orchestra musician is a tragic profession," he explains.

"He may have his own ideas on how great music ought to be played, but he never has a chance to express them. He must always play as the conductor demands it!" How does he, Joseph Krips, deal with the problem? "When I feel a certain resistance, I tell them to give their best to the *composer* — not to me!" He feels that enmity ceases to exist when he can convince the musicians that he can worthily recreate a great work of music through them. Martinon, who also believes that the enemy idea is legitimate, points out, "all my life I have been trying to fight this, and each time in front of an orchestra I try to treat them as my friends. But when you are too friendly, the musicians try to take advantage of you. They think being nice means being weak, and the discipline suffers. This creates a different psychological problem with each orchestra that you conduct."

What does it all amount to? The conductor, of course, wants to be friendly toward the musicians unless he belongs to a three-quarters extinct species that believes in nastiness for its own sake. If the musicians do not reciprocate his friendliness, either he can try to make them change their attitude, or he can ignore it and attempt to obtain the best results in spite of it. The difference is simply that if he believes in the principle of natural enmity, he will be much less concerned over the attitude of the musicians. Since it is a fact of life, he will say, you cannot influence it! If he does not believe in this principle, and he still encounters a hostile attitude, then he will probably blame himself for it.

Judging from the statements of all the conductors, whether their answer is yes or no, the problem, at least in this country, does not seem to assume such dimensions that it would seriously interfere with the accomplishments of a capable conductor. The real cause for concern will exist for the conductor who is unsure of himself and his capability and who, rather than encountering natural enmity, will generate an understandable feeling of enmity in the musicians by his ineptitude. I often wonder if the term "natural enemy" has not been coined by a disgruntled musician who spent years of his life playing under an inept conductor!

2. *In the same vein, statements such as "the Toscanini era of conducting dictators is over" may have influenced many musicians and created in their minds the image of the orchestra as a democratic institution. Do you consider this justifiable, and also, do you believe that on this basis the so-called "nice guy" of limited ability may have a better chance with some musicians than the really capable conductor who occasionally hurts their feelings?*

The reaction to this question, again not unexpectedly, is basically unanimous: it is the capable conductor who goes places with the orchestra, not the "nice guy!" Whether the Toscanini era is over or not, it is one man that must give the orders. Call it dictatorship if you will, or call it something else. But even a dictator must be reasonable in the days of strong labor unions: toughness, yes; invective and sarcasm, no!

Beyond these statements of principle that are very much in agreement with each other, there is a fascinating array of semantic problems. Barbirolli says, "to me, democracy means discipline, and in that sense the orchestra can be fully democratic." Krips thinks it should be "aristocracy, not democracy." Steinberg observes that "the player in a superior orchestra wants to be treated with friendliness but with utter strictness, and he demands to have his best values challenged at all times. This has nothing to do with dictatorship," he explains, "but it always ought to be observed that the whole system is an autocratic one. One person has to be in charge, and the others have to follow." Ehrling goes one step further when he states that "the conductor is the dictator, and has to be, because he is totally responsible for the music-making, and he cannot be responsible if he does not have authority.

Leinsdorf vehemently challenges the image of Toscanini as a dictator. "Toscanini was not a dictator," he says, "only his publicity claimed that. He often made concessions to solo players in the orchestra when their playing did not coincide with his conception of a certain phrase, as long as he felt that in each case the player's conception was convincing and musical. He tried to understand the musicians, and he did not believe that forcibly changing a good musician's interpretation would produce good results. He had flareups of temper that had to do with his background in the Italian theatre, where only the fittest (and most outspoken one!) survives, but he was not a dictator."

Explaining his own attitude toward the orchestra, Leinsdorf states that "I have been asked if it gives me a sense of power to conduct. The very opposite is true! I work with human beings, with live performers, and I must express myself through the means of their personalities." Bernstein supplies another perspective by saying "people often ask me what it must feel like to stand there and command a hundred people to do my bidding. I never know what to answer because I don't have that feeling. It seems to me that we are all doing the composer's bidding, and I am an instrument of that as much as they are. Of course," he adds, "when it comes to a disagreement on how a phrase should be played, they pay me to win that argument! But sometimes one of the musicians has an idea which I think is better than mine. In that case it costs me nothing to yield because I don't have any preconceived ideas of master and servant. It is a kind of chamber music feeling."

The "nice guy" idea is also predictably being repudiated by everyone, but with certain rather interesting limitations. Izler Solomon thinks that "a nice guy will be treated well until his lack of ability begins to irritate." Similarly, Martinon declares that "the nice guy may have a chance for one or two weeks, but no more." Steinberg injects a new idea by saying "the better the orchestra, the less chance does the nice guy have," and Rudolf dismisses the subject, stating that "the conductor must not expect to be loved, but to be respected." Elaborating on this, he observes that "a professional orchestra does not at all appreciate the chummy approach."

Unpopular as the "nice-guy" theory is, there is a readily expressed feeling of caution as to how far the conductor in rehearsal may deviate from being friendly and pleasant. "The orchestra will tolerate a certain amount of tough treatment," says Solomon, "if the musicians feel that it is based on knowledge

131

and that it will produce good results. However, toughness should always be reasonable. Sarcasm is out!" "A real sharp, chiding remark," says Rudolf, "is justified only in the case of acute lack of attention or ill will on the part of the musician." Bernstein feels that "the conductor with natural authority need not browbeat the orchestra," and Torkanowsky believes that "the important thing is the *desire* and *ability* to make good music." Barbirolli explains his own attitude by saying "if the choice is between being pleasant and losing your discipline or being unpleasant and keeping it, I am in favor of the latter!"

Consensus of opinion: the conductor must have talent, knowledge, ability and natural authority, then he does not need to be a "nice guy." On the other hand, he should keep his toughness within well established limits, otherwise he may antagonize the musicians to a point where even his capability can no longer save him!

It would have been most interesting to find out how the leading conductors in the year 1900 might have answered this question!

3. *In what manner do you think that the average musician forms his opinion of the conductor's ability, and how long does it take him to form such an opinion?*

Everyone seems agreed that this is a very fast process. "A very short time," says Leinsdorf. "Inside of fifteen minutes" (Solomon). "Before he starts to conduct" (Steinberg). "About one bar" (Bernstein). "As long as it takes a red light to change to green" (Torkanowsky). However, most conductors seem to agree that the first evaluation is not necessarily a valid or profound one. "The musicians form an opinion at once, but they correct it many times" is how Krips sees it. Rudolf goes into more detail, stating that "orchestra musicians are as apt to misjudge a conductor at first meeting as all of us do with people in daily life. However, the orchestra has an unfailing instinct for detecting during the first few minutes whether or not the conductor is a *pro*."

What are the factors that allow the musicians to make a decision so quickly, even if it is a superficial one? Is it all telepathy, as Richard Strauss' father believed, or are there other elements that enter into it?

Barbirolli thinks that the musicians know "immediately and instinctively" what the conductor's qualifications are. But he elaborates by saying that "of the qualities which they judge in a conductor, perhaps the most important one is rehearsal technique: he must be very brief and direct in his corrections." Bernstein explains that "the opinion is not formed in an intellectual way. He (the musician) knows whether you have the capacity to convey your feelings and whether you have feelings to convey." Torkanowsky opines that the musician "senses the leadership and knows whether he is comfortable under a conductor's baton." Steinberg believes that the musician's opinion is formed on the basis of "instinct and experience," but then also stresses the importance of rehearsal technique: "the player realizes immediately whether the conductor knows the essentials of what has to be rehearsed." And Solomon, somewhat more matter-of-factly, states that the main items in judging the conductor are "his knowledge of the score, his sensible rehearsal technique, and most of all, his ability to refrain from unnecessary speeches." Surprisingly, Krips is the only one who ventures the seemingly basic opinion that "the first thing the musicians expect from the conductor is a clear beat."

How valid is the opinion that is arrived at by the musicians in the first few minutes of the rehearsal? Martinon seems to feel that the musicians become more demanding in judging a conductor after they have worked with him for some time. "They see a clear beat, and they like it, but then they get accustomed to the clear beat, and they want something else. Or they feel that a conductor inspires them, and it pleases them. But then they think that he does not control them very well, and again they are displeased." Ehrling thinks that "a musician can see in a very few minutes whether a conductor knows how to conduct, technically speaking. But to find out about his musical ability would take more time, and it also varies from one musician to another. One musician may prefer the exact kind of performance, another wants the piece performed more freely. Therefore, their reactions to a conductor will differ from each other." Leinsdorf views the problem more pessimistically. According to him "the rank and file of the orchestra can quickly judge a conductor's competence, but only few musicians can judge whether what he does is musically legitimate. For example, at the end of the first movement of Brahms' First — the Meno Allegro — all the musicians can tell whether the conductor makes them feel secure going into the Meno, but only a few will know whether the amount of Meno he takes is the correct amount."

Rudolf expresses the opinion that "final evaluation of the conductor by the orchestra will only evolve in extended collaboration with him, over a long period, and even then it may differ from musician to musician." Ehrling has an interesting slant on one factor that may be responsible for the difference in opinion: "Some musicians," he explains, "the ones seated next to the conductor (concertmaster, first cellist, principal woodwinds), are more apt to find out quickly about the conductor's qualifications, more so than a violinist or a cellist at the last stand. For him it will take longer to form an opinion on account of the distance." An interesting point is also brought into this by Solomon when he mentions that "in our time in most cases the musicians have already heard about a new conductor, either by word of mouth or by advance publicity. Therefore, part of their judgment is already formed before he begins his first rehearsal." Steinberg also mentions a rather unusual aspect of what happens during the continuation of the rehearsal. He explains that "the player waits ardently for the conductor to reach the point beyond the state of affairs where the musicians are merely doing a job. He wants to find out what the conductor's method is to reach this point. The best possible solution (for the conductor) is not to let the players find out the method, so that they are simply carried along and do not know what is happening."

4. To what extent is the average orchestral musician influenced by the success (or lack of it) that the conductor may have with audience and critics?

Of the nine conductors who answered this question, six think that the musicians are not impressed by success with audience and critics, two think that they are and one does not really know. On the negative side, the strongest stand is taken by Barbirolli, who says that "if a conductor they like gets a bad review, they will say that the critic is an idiot." Rudolf agrees with this, and he adds, "If he thinks a performance was good and the public does not seem to appreciate it, he will be disappointed, but it will not lessen his respect for the conductor." Ehrling, going into more detail, explains: "The vast majority in the orchestra share the feelings of the conductor and are happy if he is successful and unhappy if he is not. If a musician enjoys the failure of his conductor, something must definitely be wrong." "I don't think orchestras have very much respect for critics," is Bernstein's opinion. "If there is a cold, unresponsive audience," he continues, "it will tell on the orchestra, but if they like what they are doing and if they trust their conductor, even the audience reaction becomes irrelevant."

Leinsdorf is on the opposite side of the fence, asserting that "they all are influenced, even if they make a solemn disclaimer." Martinon is of the same opinion, and he tells of a case where "a conductor would get on badly with the musicians, but then the success with the audience was so great that the next day the whole orchestra started to admire the conductor." Solomon asserts that "the musicians are infuriated by the conductor who uses cheap mannerisms in order to influence the audience or who distorts the music in order to get applause. They care most whether he does the right thing by the standards of the orchestra!" In Steinberg's words, "The musician does not mind the success of the conductor, as long as he is given credit for his own work." And as for audience reception, he sums up the feelings of the musicians rather intriguingly: "If it is good, it's the orchestra; if it is bad, it's the conductor!"

5. *In your opinion, should the gestures and physical behavior of the conductor change from rehearsal to performance, and if so, in what manner? What part do facial expressions play in this?*

In the answers given to this question there is an unmistakable factor of ambiguity, indicating to me that most leading conductors either are not sure what their physical actions are in performance, or that at least they are not particularly concerned. Of the nine answers, there was one definite yes (Torkanowsky), and one definite no (Krips) which was later qualified. The rest of the answers ranged from "It is not a conscious change. I merely adjust to necessities" (Barbirolli) to Steinberg's "It ought to be the same in principle. Of course it is quite possible that the presence of an audience may furnish an extra impetus to the conductor's attitude, making him give more." Solomon also thinks that "a certain amount of extra inspiration during performance can only be gained by additional gestures but not to the point where it will throw the orchestra."

Contrariwise, Bernstein is of the opinion that "the change in gesture between rehearsal and performance can be motivated by having less to do once the rehearsals are over." Similarly, Rudolf asserts that "certain desired results will necessitate more physical effort on the part of the conductor during an early rehearsal than they do later."

Martinon insists that the conductor should not "sell his possibilities to early. He should prepare the orchestra and give a little more in each rehearsal but keep

134

a reserve for the concert." As far as the amount of movement is concerned, he feels that "you do not always get intensity by physical gesture. It is the intensity from inside that will make the orchestra play with more fire." Ehrling contends that "the gestures of the conductor should not change from rehearsal to performance. This might be disturbing and make the orchestra nervous." As an exception, he allows that "perhaps in a symphony of the Vienna classics you may relax physically a little more in performance."

As for facial expressions, most conductors agree that in concert, the conductor "must preserve a certain sense of decorum" (Rudolf), and that his face should never indicate disapproval of any detail in the playing.

Torkanowsky, backing up his "yes" vote on the conductor's change of demeanor, states very graphically that "in rehearsal he should be the music director, in performance the guest conductor!" Krips, although his answer was basically no, concedes that there is one difference between rehearsal and concert: "In concert, provided that a piece has been well rehearsed, I conduct it without really listening to the playing. It is my feeling that if I listen closely and control every note that is being played, I am *behind* the orchestra. In reality, a conductor during the performance of a symphonic piece *cannot* listen! He experiences the music, and the orchestra plays his interpretation."

I was particularly impressed with this last statement. It is the kind of thing that makes you wonder why you could not have thought of it yourself! I am sure that every symphonic conductor has at one time or another noticed in performance that he was actually more interested in getting the intensity across to the orchestra than in listening to the music. Perhaps some of us have gone into self-recriminations over this, and in that light it is pleasing to hear this instinctive attitude of many of us legitimized by a man who certainly ought to know!

6. *Should the conductor in rehearsal praise or criticize the work of individual players openly, or should this be left to private confrontations?*

On this question there seems to be a substantial split of opinions. Four conductors are in favor of both praising and criticizing in public, although they all state that criticism must be constructive, never offensive, and free from sarcasm. Three others feel that praise ought to be given in public, but criticism in private. The remaining three are of the opinion that it varies with the circumstances and that no definite rule should be established.

Among the affirmative votes there is Steinberg, who states quite categorically, "I praise and criticize as the occasion demands, and I see nothing wrong with this. I am not in favor of private consultations." Bernstein thinks that "everybody learns from it." Barbirolli proposes that "every correction must be made immediately but courteously." But he cautions "never make a musician feel small! Use suggestions rather than outright criticism."

Among the in-between stands there is Ehrling, who feels that criticism may be rendered in public "if it is minor; otherwise, in private." Rudolf is of the opinion that criticism in public is justified provided that it is paired with "pertinent advice to improve the performance quickly." Leinsdorf believes "there are subjects that should only be discussed in private interviews, such as the general tendencies in a musician's playing and his possible ways of improving it. In such a case it is best if the musician takes the initiative and not the conductor!" Solomon cautions that "if the conductor will not make necessary corrections in rehearsal, the orchestra will begin to wonder whether he knows his job." About the various methods of treating musicians he explains: "There are two kinds of musicians: those who only perform well when they receive a great deal of praise and those who not only can take toughness, but actually need it in order to do their best!"

But apparently even the rendering of praise is not as harmless a matter as one might assume. Rudolf, along with at least two other conductors, stresses the point that praise should only be given when it is really deserved: "the orchestra is not a kindergarten!" And Martinon warns that there are other dangers inherent in praise: that of making other musicians jealous or that of setting an unwarranted precedent. "You praise a mediocre player who has difficulties with a certain passage in order to encourage him. But then he takes the praise for granted, and he is very hurt when you criticize him the next time!" His policy is "to behave according to the character of each player; each individual case is different!"

Altogether, one gains the impression that the various shades of opinion in this case are due to the fact that praise and criticism stem from different motivations: criticism is a matter of necessity, praise a matter of good psychology. If criticism were withheld, a nasty mistake would probably be perpetuated. But if praise were withheld, it would not make any actual difference, except perhaps in the psychological security of the player who was to be praised. Therefore, an extremely cold, matter-of-fact conductor might feel that praise is a waste of time, and he might limit all his utterances to necessary criticism. If his authority with the orchestra warranted it, he might even be successful with this method and in addition save a few minutes of rehearsal time. One thing is certain, though: such a method would in no way increase his popularity with the musicians!

7. *Do you believe that the conductor should demand performance type of playing from the very first rehearsal, or should he allow the musicians to concentrate on technical problems at first, letting the intensity of the performance evolve gradually?*

Here again, there is a considerable difference in the stated opinions, although I suspect that a substantial portion of it may be due to semantics. Some conductors state very openly that one should think of technical hurdles first and only later of intensity (Krips, Martinon, Solomon), but even the ones who believe that one ought to establish full intensity from the very first reading allow that in the case of new or difficult works this principle may have to be modified. "As long as they have not achieved the solution of technical problems, how can they perform with intensity?" asks Krips. The other extreme (perhaps!) is represented by Leinsdorf, who opines that "even with a new and unfamiliar score that is read for the first time, an effort should be made to render the music as proficiently as possible." This attitude is seconded by Steinberg, who claims that "in principle, every rehearsal must be a performance." But he cautions that this could be overdone, that "notoriously some conductors do their best work in rehearsal!"

On the side of starting with technical considerations, there is also Barbirolli, who explains that "at first I work for accuracy only. As they get to know the piece better, the intensity evolves quite naturally." And there is Torkanowsky, who muses "when you want a horse to race, you show him the track first." Ehrling compromises by saying that "in the case of a well known work it ought to be performance type of playing from the very start. Otherwise, when the work is very complicated, this cannot be done. Problems have to be solved first, and only after that can the playing be given a musical form."

Perhaps I might add something from my own experience which some of these lucky men may have forgotten since they always work with first rate orchestras: a great deal of the conductor's attitude in this problem will depend on the reading ability and flexibility of the orchestra. A work which, played by one orchestra, will sound at the first reading as if it had been rehearsed for a week will cause another orchestra all kinds of difficulties, so that with them it would be foolish for the conductor even to think of intensity at the very start!

8. *Do you demand absolute silence during rehearsals, or will you allow one group of musicians to discuss technical points among themselves while you address another group?*

This question was originally suggested to me by the statement of one of my colleagues that during the rehearsals of a certain very prominent conductor (to remain unnamed here) there was as much sound heard on stage, when the musicians were not playing, as you hear in a village cemetery at midnight! Perhaps it would be natural to assume that the greater the conductor's authority, the more silence on stage during rehearsal, but this apparently is a fallacy. As we shall see, there are other determining factors at work.

Of the ten conductors asked, three say "unconditionally yes" ("I demand absolute silence"), three say "unconditionally no," three say yes with certain exceptions, and Erich Leinsdorf says, "It depends on various factors, fatigue or nervousness of the players, for instance." He also notes that "sometimes the players want to be helpful, and such an effort should not be suppressed by the conductor. Absolute silence as a matter of principle," he says, "is nonsense." On the other hand, Steinberg declares that "any discussion has to be with me," and Krips states flatly, "No discussions!" Rudolf does not permit talk during rehearsals except in the case of a section leader addressing his section. "In such a case he is acting on my behalf." Ehrling feels that even legitimate talking could set a precedent and thus undermine the discipline, while Martinon will let the musicians talk for a few moments, and then "take the rehearsal back," reestablishing silence. Torkanowsky does not ask for absolute silence. He merely wants the musicians to be "as devoted to the task at hand as I am."

Bernstein's attitude in this matter is completely different from any of the others. He speaks of "an affectionate relationship with the orchestra," and explains "they call me Lenny, we have conversations, people are free to ask or suggest things, and it has been going on that way for many years." Of course he admits that sometimes "things get messy," and he has to be "abrupt" in order to reestablish discipline.

It is my feeling that in the matter of silence and discipline during rehearsals we are not speaking about very drastic differences between individual conductors, at least not nearly as drastic as their statements would lead one to believe! I have, at one time or another, attended rehearsals of all but one of the ten conductors interviewed, and the freedom of expression allowed the orchestra members seemed to me about equal in each case. While I do not recall any cemetery-like silence, I also do not remember a single instance where discipline seemed to be a problem and where matters threatened to get out of hand.

9. When, after some hard work during rehearsal, a difficult passage is finally played to your satisfaction, do you have it repeated immediately to make sure that its successful rendition was not an accident, or do you prefer to move on to other problems?

Really a simple question and perhaps not one of earthshaking importance. Most conductors feel that one should move on to the other problems. Two of them (Ehrling and Krips) believe that one ought to move on provided that there is a later rehearsal in which the passage can be repeated. Barbirolli and Steinberg think that it is safer to repeat at least once more. Martinon and Solomon are of the opinion that no rule can be established, that it depends on the individual case.

Leinsdorf suggests that "there must be a reason for repeating a passage, which should be stated." When there is no really concrete reason except general lack of security, he asks for one or several repeats "to get it in the fingers." Bernstein prefers to move on, except when he does not think that it was "deliberately successful." Ehrling mentions that sometimes the musicians themselves will ask for a repetition when he is already satisfied. He likes this very much because "it proves the interest the musicians show in the work they are doing."

10. Do you consider it legitimate, particularly in Classical masterworks, to solve problems of balance by making dynamic changes in the parts, or do you feel that such contingencies had better be taken care of by verbal instructions during rehearsal?

The vast majority feels that all required changes should be written into the parts. Most of them even think that the parts should be marked before the rehearsal in order to save time. Exceptions are Krips, who says, "Very rarely. The musicians must listen to each other" and Solomon, who thinks that "it is best to make the players conscious of what goes on."

The attitude of both Rudolf and Steinberg is somewhere in between. Rudolf feels that "it might be nice to have the musicians realize on their own what they must do to obtain the correct balance, but in our setup we simply have no time for this kind of thing. So I mark the parts carefully." Steinberg believes that it is good "to do as much as possible without marking" and that "in view of the ever-growing quality of American orchestras, more and more of this can be

138

done in rehearsal." However, he makes a definite exception from this principle in the works of Haydn and Mozart, where he uses his own carefully marked material. Otherwise he is of the opinion that the musicians should use the material that they are used to since "looking at unfamiliar parts may be confusing and may work against the best interests of the performance."

Ehrling is in favor of marking parts but suggests that the rehearsal be used "for fine tuning." Martinon states that he uses his own material, with everything marked in, but that on the other hand the musicians "must make their own adjustments when they play in different halls."

Barbirolli, who favors written-in changes very strongly, explains his viewpoint by saying that "the string sections have been greatly enlarged in our time (particularly in the case of works from the Viennese Classical school), and the proper balance must be restored." He explains further that "you can't leave this question of balance entirely to the players because they cannot always be sure what is the most important thing to be heard in a certain work, and it is an absolute essential for a fine and balanced performance that all the thematic material reaches the audience with complete clarity."

Leinsdorf, who says "unconditionally yes" in answer to the question, also recommends very strongly that in Beethoven's symphonies Weingartner's suggestions for such changes be studied and considered, even if not always followed to the letter.

All in all, it is very likely that most conductors, whether they approve of written-in changes or not, would go along with Barbirolli's statement that "one should be faithful to the spirit, not to the letter of the composer's work."

Chapter 13:

Evaluation of the Interviews.

Perhaps the most surprising factor encountered in the statements from these interviews is that on certain points the opinions differ so greatly from each other. How is it possible that two viewpoints are diametrically opposed to each other and yet both are legitimate?

As I have tried to point out before, the difference often rests in semantics. When there are two statements — one that says, "I demand absolute silence, except in a case where there is a legitimate problem to be discussed briefly," and another that says, "I do not demand absolute silence, and I allow the musicians to discuss their problems quietly as long as the discipline does not suffer" — one might soberly conclude that the statements are really identical, despite the fact that one answers the question with yes, and the other with no. In another case, there is no noticeable difference between saying "I demand performance type of playing from the very first reading, except when a contemporary or otherwise unusually difficult work makes a different approach necessary," or "I believe in solving technical problems first and letting the intensity evolve gradually, except in the case of familiar classical works, where such an approach is unnecessary." Again the positive and the negative answer come very close to agreeing with each other.

Music, after all, is an art and not a science, and a certain ambiguity, not to say vagueness, is suggested by its very material. I do not believe that in any such case the inference should be drawn that one answer is absolutely right and the other absolutely wrong. They are merely the reactions of different personalities, each of them legitimate on its own grounds.

The only limitation that could perhaps be made concerning the validity of a few statements is that some conductors who are very eloquent on the podium do not communicate nearly as well in their verbal statements. (Incidentally, the opposite can also be true!)

The reader who perhaps expected some completely new and shattering revelations from these interviews may possibly be disappointed. If that is the case, I can sympathize with his viewpoint, but I shall respectfully disagree with it. Probably not every sentence that I have quoted is an absolutely incomparable pearl of wisdom. Still, some conductors happily are every bit as convincing with the word as they are with the baton. When I look at a statement such as that by Josef Krips, about the conductor not really listening during performance, that by William Steinberg about not allowing the musician to find out the conductor's method, Leinsdorf's enlightening exploration of the phenomenon of Toscanini, or in a lighter vein, Bernstein's saying that he is paid to win the argument, then I feel rather richly rewarded for whatever effort it took to obtain these interviews.

Perhaps the reader will feel rewarded, too, (or at least consoled for the absence of whatever oracular pronouncements he expected to find!) when he realizes that probably never before — to quote Churchill very freely and inappropriately — have so many leading conductors said so much about conducting in so few pages.

The results that these men obtain in their work are well known. But their underlying ideas and self-described methods may well furnish a stimulant to the student or to the less experienced professional.

Epilogue.

When all has been said — all that we should know about conducting and **its** various aspects, all that can be of help to us in the mastery of its technical, musical and psychological components — there is still one question that remains unanswered: why is it that among two dozen performances of a Classical symphony there is usually one that leaves all others far behind? Why can we listen to eight recordings of an opera, express approval of all of them and then find one that stuns us, one that impels us to say, "This is the way the composer would have liked to hear his music performed!"? What makes us genuinely admire twelve interpretations and then turns the thirteenth into an overwhelming spiritual experience?

Needless to say, it is the imagination and depth of vision of the conductor. But why? What causes one man to do things with a score that by far overshadow the accomplishments of his most significant rivals?

All of us who are interested in symphony and opera performances have at one time or another tried to find a solution to this puzzle with varying degrees of success. But then suddenly something happens which almost forcibly suggests the answer that we have been trying to find. It was perhaps a dozen years ago that I attended the performance of a Beethoven symphony played by one of the top-ranking orchestras and conducted by a man whose name is highly respected all over the world. It was an extremely neat and clean performance, and the sound was excellent. The tempi were absolutely correct, and even the most zealous purist could not have found fault with dynamics or phrasing. Yet the whole thing left me curiously cold and unsatisfied. The notes were there, properly executed, the style was there, and yet Beethoven did not speak to me that night. Suspecting that my own mood might have been to blame, I questioned several musically erudite and sensitive friends who had also heard the performance. Their reactions were no different from my own.

I became very preoccupied. Ordinarily, when one is displeased with the performance of a Classical symphony, it is easy to say, "The opening was too fast. In the Allegro there was not enough dynamic contrast. The slow movement did not sing enough. The tempo transition in the finale began too late and was too abrupt, etc." But not in this case! There was nothing that one could criticize: nothing was really wrong, but the whole thing was *not right*.

Then I started to think about the personality of the conductor. Of his technical mastery there could be no doubt. Nor could there be any doubt of his thorough knowledge of the Classical literature and its style and his vast experience in conducting standard symphonic works. Probing further in my own mind, I remembered that several people had told me how they disliked the man personally, that he was vain, egotistical, rather shallow and primitive in his extra-musical taste, and even in music perhaps chiefly interested in his own personal success.

I thought about this, and — possibly by process of free association — my memory took me back another ten years to the time when I was one of the

142

assistants in the opera productions at the Met that Bruno Walter conducted at that time. I remembered how Bruno Walter rehearsed *Orfeo, Don Giovanni* and *Fidelio*. I heard him speak to the performers, patiently pleading with them to do justice to the spiritual essence of the work, to try to feel everything that was in it. There was no vanity in his words, no egotism, only a deeply sincere re-experiencing of the composer's message. No one remained untouched. He made us want to mourn with the bereaved Orpheus and to jubilate with the liberated prisoners in *Fidelio*. Here was a man who did not seek popularity, and yet, everyone loved him, was ready to make sacrifices for him and felt purified by his presence.

And then back to the other conductor. Could he have purified people by his presence, could he have met the great composers on their home territory, the way Bruno Walter did? Of course not. You cannot give spiritual elevation to others unless your own spirit is elevated. There is a certain type of music-making that has its roots not merely in great musicianship, but in the profound qualities that distinguish a great human being. To possess these qualities it is not necessary to be a great composer like Mahler or Strauss, nor to be a man of great universal erudition like Walter, Furtwängler or Weingartner. The Toscaninis and Monteuxs have their own ways of greatness. But one thing is certain: the vain, the shallow and the self-centered can never achieve it. They may be very skillful technicians and extremely capable interpreters of the text. But they lack one quality: the human depth of a Walter or a Toscanini that made these men what they were and that comes across even in many of their recordings; in short, that forms the basis of the listener's spiritual experience.

Could this be the answer?

Bibliography

Antek, Samuel, *This Was Toscanini*. New York, Vanguard Press, 1963.

Bamberger, Carl, *The Conductor's Art*. New York, McGraw-Hill, 1965.

Berlioz, Hector, *The Orchestral Conductor, Theory of His Art*. New York, Fischer, 1929.

Blaukopf, Kurt, *Great Conductors*. London, Arco Publishers Limited, 1955.

Boult, Adrian, *Thoughts on Conducting*. London, Phoenix House, 1963.

Busch, Fritz, *Der Dirigent*. Zürich, Atlantis-Verlag, 1961.

Chotzinoff, Samuel, *Toscanini, an Intimate Portrait*. New York, Knopf, 1956.

Ewen, David, *Dictators of the Baton*. Chicago, Alliance Book Corp., 1943.

Furtwängler, Wilhelm, *Concerning Music*. London, Boosey & Hawkes, 1953.

Gillis, Daniel, *Furtwängler Recalled*. Tuckahoe, N. Y., John de Graff, 1964.

Grosbayne, Benjamin, *Techniques of Modern Orchestral Conducting*. Cambridge, Mass., Harvard Univ. Press, 1956.

Krueger, Karl, *The Way of the Conductor*. New York, Charles Scribner's Sons, 1958.

Malko, Nikolai, *The Conductor and His Baton*. Copenhagen, Hansen, 1950.

McElheran, Brock, *Conducting Technique for Beginners and Professionals*. New York, Oxford Univ. Press, 1966.

Mueller, John H., *The American Symphony Orchestra*. Bloomington, Ind,. Indiana Univ. Press, 1951.

Munch, Charles, *I Am a Conductor*. New York, Oxford Univ. Press, 1955.

Rudolf, Max, *The Grammar of Conducting*. New York, G. Schirmer, 1950.

Scherchen, Hermann, *Handbook of Conducting*. New York, Oxford Univ. Press, 1942.

Schmid, Adolf, *The Language of the Baton*. New York, G. Schirmer, 1937.

Steinberg, William, *Conducting, a Human Occupation*. "International Musician," 1966, an interview with Hope Stoddard.

Stoessel, Albert, *The Technique of the Baton*. New York, Carl Fischer, 1928.

Wagner, Richard, *Uber das Dirigieren*, Vol. 8 of *Sämtliche Schriften und Dichtungen*, Leipzig, Breitkopf & Härtel, 1911.

Walter, Bruno, *Of Music and Music-Making*. New York, W. W. Norton, 1961.

Weingartner, Felix, *On Conducting* (trans. Newman). New York, Kalmus, n.d.

Weissmann, Adolf, *Der Dirigent im 20. Jahrhundert*. Berlin, Propylaen-Verlag, 1925.

Wilhelm Furtwängler's Briefe, Wiesbaden, F. A. Brockhaus, 1964.

145